ISBN 978-1-331-55390-8
PIBN 10205118

1 MONTH OF
FREE
READING

at

www.ForgottenBooks.com

By purchasing this book you are eligible for one month membership to ForgottenBooks.com, giving you unlimited access to our entire collection of over 700,000 titles via our web site and mobile apps.

To claim your free month visit:

www.forgottenbooks.com/free205118

Similar Books Are Available from
www.forgottenbooks.com

THE HOME LIFE
OF SWINBURNE

BY

CLARA JANE WATTS-DUNTON

LONDON
A. M. PHILPOT
69 GREAT RUSSELL STREET
1922

COPYRIGHT

CAHILL AND CO., LTD., LONDON, DUBLIN AND DROGHEDA.

TO

THE LADY ARCHIBALD CAMPBELL OF ARGYLL

THE LOYAL FRIEND OF SWINBURNE AND WATTS-DUNTON,

THIS BOOK IS AFFECTIONATELY DEDICATED

BY THE AUTHOR.

PREFATORY NOTE

THREE of the chapters of " The Home Life of Swinburne " have appeared as articles in the *Nineteenth Century and After.* I have to tender my thanks to the editor of that magazine for his permission to reprint them.

C. W. D.

CONTENTS

ILLUSTRATIONS

CHAPTER I

FIRST VISIT TO THE PINES

My mother, Mrs. Reich, met Watts-Dunton when I was a girl at school, and they were friends almost at once. She was a woman of fine musical ability besides being a keen judge of books and their authors, and she became a visitor at The Pines, Putney Hill, where Swinburne and his devoted friend resided. I was sixteen years of age when my mother took me to visit Mr. Watts—as Watts-Dunton was then called. In a chapter contributed to his biography I have described that visit and the wonderful change in my life which it preluded. It was the first step—little though I dreamed it—that led to my marriage to the great critic and brought me into domestic relationship with Algernon Charles Swinburne. I did not, however, see Swinburne on the occasion of my first visit to The Pines. A whole year elapsed

15

before I was formally presented to the greatest English poet of his day.

Exactly a week after this first visit a note came to my mother from Mr. Watts asking if we " would like to come and dine with Swinburne and me." It may, perhaps, be conjectured that this invitation thrilled me at least as much as my mother's proposal of the week before · " I am going to take you to meet my friend Mr. Watts." As a matter of fact, the contrary was the case. The presence of the famous poet would, it seemed to me, interfere with the delightful flow of my newly-found friend's conversation. From my first visit I had come away in an ecstasy of admiration and exultation. I had gone merely pleased with the idea of meeting the author of a work which I loved—the sonnet sequence on the Fausts of Berlioz, Gounod and Schumann. I had come away with a warm regard for the man. Until I met him again I lived in a state of longing anticipation. My school-lessons were neglected or forgotten in tribute to that unmistakable and arresting gift of personality which was his in marvellous measure. School-girl though I was, I could discern in him the divine gift of genius, and I had no desire to meet his famous friend since I found himself so satisfying.

FIRST VISIT TO THE PINES

In fact, an uncomfortable feeling of shyness came over me at the idea of meeting Swinburne. It was not that I feared to experience any sort of *mauvaise honte*, for I had no lack of the self-possession required by people unknown to fame on being presented to a celebrity. The fact was that at this juvenile period of my existence, Swinburne's poetry was " caviare " to me if not to " the general," and I imagined he would expect me to know a great deal about it—in fact, to be a profound Swinburnian, though my actual excursions into the realms of his Muse had covered very little ground. It is true my Canadian governess at school had read to me portions of " Songs before Sunrise," and was never tired of telling me of the wonderful effect " Atalanta " had produced upon her when in 1865 she read this masterpiece for the first time in far-away Toronto. She would recite to me bits from the choruses, and I became quite accustomed to hearing her declaim at odd moments in a voice throbbing with a sense of their beauty that soul-stirring lyric which begins—

When the hounds of spring are on winter's traces,
  The mother of months in meadow or plain
Fills the shadows and windy places
  With lisp of leaves and ripple of rain.

B   17

Often during our walk she would carry with her to read under the trees while the girls played rounders or tennis a volume of Swinburne in an American edition, the outside cover of which grew quite familiar to me. It was " Laus Veneris," the work now generally known as " Poems and Ballads." She would sit reading it, entirely absorbed and lost in its pages ˙and oblivious of everything around her. If during a halt in our game I came near her to rest for a while, up would go her finger to admonish silence and a gentle " Sh—Sh ! " would issue from her half-parted lips. When it was time to return to the house she would cause me to walk beside her, and then I would hear about " Anactoria " and other of the glorious pieces to be found within the covers of her cherished volume. She prized her " Laus Veneris " very much, and had brought it with her from America. She was fond of telling me how eagerly after reading "Atalanta in Calydon " she had seized upon it when it first came out. But she never told me of the *succès du scandale* which its appearance evoked, although she must have known all about it. A good deal of water had to flow under London Bridge before I could put before the reader this interesting evidence of one of Swinburne's friends—then resident in

FIRST VISIT TO THE PINES

Boston, U.S.A.—of the extraordinary sensation " Laus Veneris " caused in America in 1866.

Dec. 2nd, 1866.

To Algernon Swinburne, Pagan, suffering persecution from the Christians . . . greeting.

You may have already heard, mon cher, that your book is making a furore in this continent. No new volume of Tennyson has ever made more talk. . . . The publisher has sold 6,000 and is now printing the seventh. Mr. Emerson, to whom I was introduced yesterday, asked me a great many questions about you. He had read your " Madonna Mia " detached and instantly got the book.

Lowell, he said (" Biglow Papers " Lowell) being a linguist was especially interested in that department of your brain, his curiosity having been excited about your Greek verses and French songs.

I have just read Fraser's article—it is very fair. Longfellow was out when I called so I have not seen him. I am going back to New York to-morrow and I suppose I shall not return for some time. I shall very probably pass a year in that city and so finish my medical studies. You were good enough to say you wanted to read my African book which I promised to send you, but never did—because I thought to do something better with the old materials. This I am going to work on now. It will be published at first only in America—I will send you a copy.

Give my regards to our mutual friends and believe me,

Yours truly,

WINWOOD READE.*

* William Winwood Reade (1838-1875) was a nephew of Charles Reade and the author of " The Martyrdom of Man," " Savage Africa," etc.

THE HOME LIFE OF SWINBURNE

In spite of all this admiration on the part of my governess for the poetry of Swinburne, Byron continued to be my pet poet, and I never attempted to explore for myself the verse of this far greater singer. Consequently, having so meagre a knowledge of Swinburne the Poet, I was intimidated by the prospect of dining with Swinburne the man, and without considering what an honour had been paid me, I asked my mother to make some excuse for declining the invitation. I horribly wanted to go, but I was dominated by the idea that Swinburne would turn out to be that pet aversion of Don Juan—

> An author that's *all author*, a fellow
> In foolscap uniform turned up with ink.

I had lately been reading " Don Juan," and was passing through that stage of adulation for my unsaintly hero which is the prerogative of many young people of a romantic tendency. I was never tired of airing emancipated and laudatory opinions regarding the poetry of Byron, and "Don Juan " in particular, to my governess. Being a real lover of poetry, she fostered any tastes in this direction among such of the girls as cared for poetry at all; she was even something of a poet herself. Far from putting a check on my predilection for " Don Juan " she invited me to dip into the precious " Laus Veneris " myself. So deep and sincere was her admiration for Swinburne that " Dolores " and " Faustine " were by no manner of means anathema to her, nor were they "forbidden fruit " to me. On the contrary, being an exceptionally broad-minded woman, she even encouraged me to read them. Whether I would have understood them is quite another thing. However, I had not read them, and my knowledge of Byron was of course of no use as a substitute, especially as I had received what I considered a great ' set back ' when, on venturing to remark to Mr. Watts that I considered Byron equal to Shakespeare, he replied · " I dare say he is at your age." Naturally I thought that perhaps Swinburne might not prove so kind.

It would be just as well, I reflected, to allow time enough to elapse for my mind to be less inadequately equipped with a knowledge of Swinburne, not to mention a few other poets, before I went through the ordeal of a dinner with him. I wondered what fantastic whim could have induced Fortune to set her wheel moving in my direction, when just one turn more might have passed me by, and offered my opportunity to some-one far more deserving. Had it been possible, I would ungrudgingly have yielded my place in the

Sun to any one of the scores of Swinburnian enthusiasts who were so immeasurably more fitted than
I to profit by such luck. I felt quite sorry that my
poor governess could not change places with me ;
she would not have felt on the horns of a dilemma.

In the end I persuaded my mother to intimate
my intention of calling at The Pines on the same
evening appointed for dining with the two friends,
but after dinner. By going after dinner I
imagined I should be free to talk *tête-á-tête* to
Mr. Watts, whom I shall henceforth call Walter,
and that my explanation would be accepted in the
right way. I felt he would listen to all I had to
say with correct and real understanding. I was
right in my surmise, for when I arrived at his
house, at about eight-thirty, dinner was over, and
he was alone, waiting to receive me in his charming
dining-room which, contrary to a published
account, is not connected by folding doors with the
adjoining room.

Almost the first object which caught my eye was
the particularly beautiful mantelpiece, and as this
work of art has been very erroneously described by
a distinguished writer, I think it would not be
amiss to give an accurate description of it. The
mantelpiece, which is one of two exactly alike, the
other being in the drawing-room, was made at the

oldest pottery in England—John Dwight's, established in 1671. They are made of glazed stoneware in lovely shades of blue and buff. They have been admired by every artist who has seen them, including no less a person than William Morris, and there are none like them in existence, as their production, though very original and charming, was found too expensive to be profitable.

It was a lovely summer evening and Walter suggested we should stroll out into the garden. He invited me to partake of the biggest, fattest gooseberries I had ever seen that were weighing down the bushes. But I was far too happy and excited to eat, and our talk which had begun at our auspicious meeting of the preceding Monday was resumed with a delightful freedom from restraint. He received all my small remarks on music and poetry and books with such patience and interest that I was sure my explanation with regard to Swinburne would be quite safe in his keeping.

" Why did you not want to come to dinner ? " he asked. " I told Swinburne he was to expect an ardent champion of ' Don Juan,' and *I* knew what a refreshing surprise he would receive when he met it in the person of yourself—tell me the reason why you did not turn up? "

I felt no hesitation in telling him I would rather

wait until I had read "Poems and Ballads" before I met the author. He seemed particularly amused at this explanation, and tried hard to grasp the meaning behind my words, but I failed to make him understand why I felt Swinburne would be aghast at my limitations, and that if I talked to him about "Don Juan" and omitted to speak of "Poems and Ballads" he would think me a dreadful little ignoramus.

Instead of taking me seriously—and I was terribly in earnest at the time—he treated this latter portion of my confession as a huge joke. He laughed so long and so heartily that I wondered with dismay what stupid thing I could have said. I begged him to tell why he was laughing. He either could not, or would not tell me, but wanted instead to carry me off and make me known to Swinburne there and then. But I was too engrossed in the exhilarating company of my friend to desire any interruptions. To walk about in such a charming garden listening to the conversation of my host was the greatest of treats to me. It was impossible to be long in his company without learning something from his rich scholarship or without becoming aware that his mind was a veritable storehouse. Far from his being obtrusively "bookish," there was a sympathetic giving of himself that actually made you imagine *he* was learning from *you,* instead of its being the other way about. That magnetic power which attracted so many to him won from me an instinctive response. It was delicious to be in this cool, pretty garden surrounded on all sides by big shady trees, its high walls completely covered with thick ivy. From his study window overhead, Swinburne could look out on a perfect forest of green, and enjoy quite a striking view, for the large trees in the background conveyed a sense of space and a feeling of distance which was not so apparent in the foreground where I stood. We stayed chatting until it grew dusk. The time had flown so swiftly that I had no idea how late it was till the arrival of a maid, sent by my mother to claim me, put an end to our delightful talk.

When at the garden gate Walter said " au revoir " with the assurance that we had many more such meetings to look forward to, I felt somewhat reconciled to the approach of the dreaded Monday which would see me back again at my desk and lesson-books. As we shook hands, I told him once again I felt really shy at the idea of meeting Swinburne, and meant every word I had said. But he waived all my scruples to one side with the remark that he knew I was joking. With a confident and reassuring smile he concluded · " All right then ; it shall be as you wish, but you need not be afraid to meet Swinburne—you are sure to like him ; if you feel you are not quite ready to meet him, tell me when you think you are, and I know at your first meeting all your fears will be at an end "—adding, however, in a tone meant to be quite reassuring, that " Poems and Ballads " would be about the last thing their author would expect me to discuss or talk about to him. He also said that if I " let myself go " on the amusing subject of " Don Juan," Swinburne would only be refreshed.

I returned to school very full of my adventures of the week-end and brimming over with enthusiasm at the success of my garden talk.

This was tremendous news to tell my Swinburnian governess. She was profoundly interested in all I had to tell her. Our walk that Monday was marked with a white stone. In spite of its being a " French morning," when all one's talk with her had to be in French, I insisted on walking with her both to and from the " garden," as we called the school's recreation ground. Instead of wishing to " shunt " the exercise of that language by walking with one of the girls, I opened the ball myself by suggesting, "*Puis-je marcher avec vous ce matin, chèrie?*" I was bubbling over with excitement, and in my indifferent French kept up a flow of reminiscent talk, knowing I was pouring it all into a ready and sympathetic ear. I can hear the interested tones of her voice now as she asks some question : "*Je suppose que M. Swinburne?*" or : "*Est-ce que M. Watts vous a dit?*"

With such an exceptionally happy start, I was not going to allow the grass to grow under my feet in acquiring all the knowledge I could about Swinburne's poetry. I was fired by the desire to become acquainted with "Poems and Ballads," and for a year—in the interval of lessons—I read nearly everything of Swinburne's I could lay hands on. I was determined when I met him that he should not find me the proverbial " Miss " of Byronic satire, who " always smells of bread and butter."

Swinburne at this time had just completed "The Tale of Balen," and Walter, thinking it would please me to see the handwriting of the Bard (as A. C. S. was often styled and as I shall often style him) gave me the MS. to read. Perceiving also that my writing was clear enough to prove " a bit of fat " for the printers, he asked me to make a copy of Swinburne's MS., so that my copy could go to be set up in type.

THE HOME LIFE OF SWINBURNE

This was the first occasion that my eyes lighted on the familiar blue paper on which Swinburne invariably wrote. As I transferred his words to my foolscap I noticed how very perfect the MS. was : there were hardly any revisions : it seemed to me that the whole long poem *must* have simply flowed from his pen. But what struck me most was the singular boyishness of the handwriting, which despite its appearance of youth, was well-formed and particularly characteristic. One could imagine it to be the writing of a schoolboy of thirteen or fourteen, so distinct and easy to read was every word. Every up-stroke and down-stroke of his beautifully neat letters suggested the firm writing of a boy with the mechanism of mind and body in perfect order.

How proud I felt to be given this task, and very carefully did I copy the great poet's words in my big round hand, never dreaming as I did so that one day I myself would play my part in the home life of these two inseparable companions.

But perhaps even as I copied the first stanza of " Balen," some fairy knew that years later I would be literally dancing to its measure in the company of him who wrote it.

CHAPTER II

EARLY IMPRESSIONS

AFTER this garden-talk Walter and I were constantly in each other's society and I was so often a visitor to The Pines that my encounters with Swinburne were frequent. I would meet him in the hall or the passages, and although he did not appear to see me, he would stand like a sentinel while I passed ; his arms stiff against his sides, with the palms presented outwards, gave him a curiously mechanical appearance—as of a toy-soldier. On these occasions I felt somewhat overawed, for Swinburne would look at me with such a wondering look, as much as to say—" Who are you, and what are you doing here?" Then he would bow very courteously, and disappear into his room.

Late one afternoon in winter when the snow was on the ground and all was cold and dreary outside, I happened to be passing his room, and looking in upon him through the half-open door, I saw him seated by the fire with a book in his hand. He was laughing over something he was reading and gave little gurgles of delight. It all looked so delightfully cosy, with the curtains drawn, the big fire burning, and Swinburne sitting near it, looking so blithe and gay, that, wondering what he had found in the book to make him feel so jolly, I thought, for a moment, I must go in and ask him. Of course I did *not* go in, but I went downstairs and told Walter I felt tempted to do so. He seemed quite pleased, and suggested that the next day Swinburne and I should make our first salutation. Accordingly, the following afternoon Walter took me upstairs into the Bard's sanctum and there at last we became known to each other.

Swinburne was reading when we came into the room, and seeing who had entered, he laid the book aside, face downwards, and came forward with extended hand to meet me.

One might have supposed that my former encounters would have made my face somewhat familiar to him, since all the details of his physiognomy were indelibly stamped on my mental vision. But it was not so; he appeared to be meeting me for the first time. As he gave me one of his old-world bows, I felt he really had never noticed me before that day. The poet then drew forward a chair, and with somewhat elaborate politeness, invited me to sit down. Then from the depths of a dark recess in a corner he drew forth a wonderful-looking volume—he must have known just where to put his hand on it even in the dark, for the room was full of shadows, and illuminated only by candles. He hugged it gleefully to him, and in a boyish ringing voice exclaimed : " Now I am going to show you something that will surprise you. I wager you've never seen such a book as this." And indeed it was a most remarkable book, the like of which I had never seen before.

He brought his chair close to mine, and opening a page at random, he pointed to the most extra-ordinary specimen of the feathered tribe. As far as the body and beak were concerned, this " bird " did not belie its name, but the creature appeared to possess a neck far more like that of a giraffe than anything else. The head was so curious, too, and in its eye was a most audacious twinkle. Swinburne pointed to this impossible neck with delight, and excitedly asked " Did you ever see such a bird as that in your life? " He spoke in what I can only describe as an angelically kinder-garten manner. I thought that perhaps he had under-estimated my age by a decade, for, ignorant of the rarity and antiquarian interest of the book I imagined that it was a book for children of tender years, for whose delectation the poet was wont to exhibit it. As he obviously expected me to reply in equally emphatic language, I replied that I certainly had never seen such a queer-looking bird before, and never dreamed such a one had even existed. " But is it really supposed to be a *bird* ?" I asked.

" Oh, yes," said Swinburne, very earnestly. " I never for moment hazarded such a doubt,"

I *had* to believe it then. But noticing there was a verse underneath the picture which might give me a key to the riddle, I turned to the page again and tried to read it. This was beyond me, for the type in which it was written was almost impossible for me to decipher. I asked Swinburne to read it to me : he instantly complied, and in the most amusing rhyme it is possible to imagine, I was given the description and veritable history of his mysterious " bird." The book was made up of the queerest creatures of natural history, and the next page revealed yet another weird specimen which made me know at once that Swinburne had been playing a practical joke on me in allowing me to imagine in the first instance that the animals illustrated were like anything in heaven or on earth.

In the most ingratiating manner he proceeded to show me what professed to be a cat. The Bard's face was wreathed in smiles as he exclaimed, " Oh, but do look at this. What a dear creature !"

The " dear creature " had a human face, and rather an ugly face, too, I thought. Being anxious to know if this four-footed specimen of creation was of the male or female gender, I again requested Swinburne to read from the verse underneath. He was overjoyed to do so, but unfortunately we failed to arrive at any definite conclusion —although this rhymed description was even funnier than the one about the " bird." When I suggested that this ambiguous grimalkin was possibly a woman, Swinburne was quite ready to fall in with my idea, and laughingly said, "Ah, you are right; *yes*, of course, it's pretty certain to be a woman."

The volume containing these pictures was really a fragment of a much larger book, and one of the very earliest illustrated volumes ever printed. I think Swinburne said it was about four hundred years old. I am sorry to say I cannot remember its name. Perhaps some of my readers will identify it from my description. I may add that the pictures included a man-headed serpent of repellent visage, a mermaid with a smiling countenance, sirens of alluring appearance, grotesque camels and impossibly-formed monkeys. Each creature was the subject of a descriptive stanza so ludicrous that it was difficult for Swinburne to read it without laughing outright.

One or two of the pages were torn here and there. Supposing it might have been the youthful Algernon who had mutilated them, I enquired if he had done so when he was a little boy.

He looked quite pained, and said he was thankful he had not committed such a heinous offence, but he suspected that some naughty little child hundreds and hundreds of years ago was the culprit.

I really think Swinburne prized this blackletter fragment more than any other book in his valuable library. He treated it with a reverence which did not escape my notice. I could see he was very nervous at my handling it, and preferred to turn the leaves himself. He said in a touching voice, full of quiet pathos, " My dear mother gave me this book."

By this time the feeling of shyness and awe with which the poet had hitherto inspired me was dispelled. I began to feel quite at home in his company, and thoroughly at my ease. I wanted to tell him I had read " The Tale of Balen," and when there was a pause in the conversation, I told him how much I had enjoyed reading this poem. He seemed delighted to hear me say so, and said : " Have you though?   I am very pleased you like it."

Knowing he was a Northumbrian, I thought perhaps he might be interested to hear I knew well the rugged beauties of Northumberland, and was familiar with that part of the coast in which " Balen " is laid.   When I told him this, he was still more delighted.   But when I proceeded to add that I, too, was a Northumbrian, and was born and had spent my early childhood by the sea within twenty miles of Capheaton, he was quite astonished, and a French locution, ever afterwards to be associated in my mind with him, escaped from his lips.   Looking hard at me out of those wonderful eyes, he ejaculated two or three times the word " *Tiens* ! "

On a table at my elbow near where I was sitting, I could read the title of the book he had been reading when we came in.   It was " Uncle Bernac " by Conan Doyle.   Taking the volume up, I asked Swinburne if it was exciting and if he had ever read " The Adventures of Sherlock Holmes."

THE HOME LIFE OF SWINBURNE

He ignored my first question, but answered the second by repeating in large capitals, "HAVE I READ 'THE ADVENTURES OF SHERLOCK HOLMES'? RATHER! Ask Walter." The two friends exchanged glances, and loud guffaws followed the torrent of reminiscent talk regarding the miraculous intuitive and deductive powers of the epoch-making detective, whom the poet considered a " marvellous man," and pronounced a " great lark." It seems that in common with nearly every schoolboy in the kingdom, as well as thousands of people of both sexes who are no longer at school, he had revelled vicariously in the experiences of his " marvellous" friend. He told me he had read every adventure as they appeared in the *Strand Magazine*, and that he liked nothing better than a good detective story; the more thrilling the better he liked it. I said I had gone through the same phase myself, and had read and enjoyed most of the "Adventures." Then turning to me he enquired: "But have you read 'The Sign of Four,' and 'A Study in Scarlet?' I warrant these two stories will not disappoint you, and will provide you with all the 'thrills' you want."

I told him I had not done so, but, if they were half as interesting as some of Sherlock Holmes'

Adventures, I would certainly take his advice and read them.

I never imagined that my answer in the negative would result in my becoming the possessor of these books in a most charming way.

'At the conclusion of my delightful little visit, Swinburne urged me to come as often as I liked to "look at the animal book," and told me that when I came again he would show me some of his rare first editions of the Dramatists. I assured him I would soon avail myself of his invitation, and with another gracious bow at departure, and a cordial hand-shake, we bade each other good afternoon and "au revoir." I was charmed with him, and when Walter and I went downstairs I told him that never again should I be nervous with Swinburne.

Looking over that book with him, I felt that we were contemporaries, and that I had spent the afternoon in the company of a brilliant, intellectual and enthusiastic boy, so young was he in heart and spirit. He looked so full of life and vigour that one forgot his years, such light was in his eyes, such warmth in his smile, and he seemed so blissfully happy, surrounded by his thousands of books which lined the room from floor to ceiling.

This lithe, energetic man of genius literally

radiated happiness. His whole environment spoke of the peace of mind and harmony of life which had been his from the moment he had set foot within The Pines.

The almost adoring expression which came into Swinburne's eyes when they looked at Walter made me realize how deeply and gratefully conscious he was of the incalculable blessing the magnetic presence of his friend had been to him all the happy years he had spent under his roof. Owing to Walter's vigilance and his interposition between the poet and the interfering prose of life—which would have spelt damnation to Swinburne's art and temperament—the latter was enabled to bring forth his later immortal works. In this atmosphere of repose and freedom from worry, one felt that Time had nothing to do with him, and that he might go on living and working for ever.

Walter's self-effacement surprised me then and astonished me later. The tender solicitude and unremitting care which he lavished upon Swinburne, heedless of his own sacrifice of strength and leisure for artistic achievement so long as he furthered the welfare of " the dear fellow," as he sometimes called the Bard, are unparalleled in the annals of literary friendships.

CHAPTER III

" THAT ' LIMBER ELF ' "

FOR some time I had had access to Walter's library,
—a literary workshop that contained upwards of
eight thousand volumes. Books were everywhere,
towering from floor to ceiling ; they filled immense
bookcases and little bookcases, and occupied every
table and chair in the room and nearly all the
available floor-space besides. The effect of this
mountain of tomes all around me was somewhat
staggering until I got used to it, then it actually
grew upon me, and I became so accustomed to the
delightful disorder that I was quite miserable when
the day came for tidying up. All you had to
do was to stand in the middle of it all, and
after surveying it calmly, shut your eyes,
and then make a random bee-line with your
finger for a book and trust that this childish
method of procedure would bring you the luck

of "Little Jack Horner" when he pulled out a plum.

This was invariably my habit when let loose among Walter's books, and it nearly always brought a plum to me.

So lucky was I in hitting upon some unusual volume amidst this heterogeneous collection that I earned for myself the sobriquet of "limber elf." Walter declared this almost uncanny method—or rather want of method—so productive of special "finds" which I never set out to obtain— reminded him of the child in Coleridge's "Christabel"—

> A little child, a limber elf,
> Singing, dancing to itself—
> A fairy thing with red round cheeks,
> That always finds, and never seeks.

One day I lighted on a volume which instantly riveted me. I knew at once that I had "struck oil" and had stumbled across something of more than common interest.

It was a presentation book to Walter from Swinburne, and at the beginning was written in the poet's handwriting a sonnet on Massinger. And—delightful discovery—this was a book of plays, and I loved reading plays. I looked eagerly through it to find "A New Way to Pay Old Debts," the name of which I knew well. Ever since hearing this delightful title at school during one of our weekly lectures on literature, I had wanted to read this play, but so far I had never had an opportunity of doing so. I was naturally overjoyed to see it here in print before my eyes, and immediately began to devour it. So interested did I become in its pages that I was unaware of the presence of Walter at my elbow. His " What has that ' limber elf ' got hold of now?" brought me back to my surroundings. He was highly amused at my seizing upon this particular book among the thousands in the room. Handing him the volume that had so absorbed me, I asked him to tell me about it, for I was anxious to know why Swinburne had written this sonnet in his inscribed copy. Latterly I had heard so much about Swinburne's interesting quartos that I was considerably puzzled and wanted to know just exactly what they were. Walter did not at once answer my question, but told me to take care of the Massinger while he hunted round himself in order to show me the other copies of Elizabethan plays which Swinburne had given him. He soon discovered some others—I forget now which they were, though I know there was a Ben

Jonson, but I remember that in each Swinburne had written a eulogistic and impassioned sonnet addressed to the author and redolent of intense hero-worship.

Then Walter told me about his friend's adoration of the Elizabethan dramatists, and his profound knowledge on the subject, and prepared me for the feast that was awaiting me when I went to see the poet's collection of first editions.

This made me even more eager to finish reading "A New Way to Pay Old Debts," which the entrance of Walter had interrupted. I found the play so intensely interesting that I was impatient to go on with it, so after he had carefully put away the other plays in a place of safety, he left me to continue my fascinating pursuit.

Perhaps I may be excused for telling a story of my school days, bearing on Massinger's famous play.

Every time I was in arrears over my monthly debts to the school fine-box the title of this play would roll glibly off my tongue. It became a sort of by-word in my mouth, for I delighted in the very sound of the words—which I used on every pretext—and I detested to pay up. My fines far exceeded those of any of the other girls, and when my "bad marks," which cost the large sum of a penny each, were added up at the beginning of every month, I never had enough money to pay in full. Then out would come this very appropriate title.

To get out of the difficulty I would ask to have the debt "carried over" to the next month. My governess, who was really quite fond of me never insisted on my paying up to the last fraction, or thereby I should have been bereft of pocket-money for the whole of the ensuing month. According to what sort of temper she happened to be in at the time, she would allow me to pay so much "on account." My usual average was about two or three "bad marks" a day, and at the end of one term I was asked, I remember, to pay my arrears to the tune of eighteen shillings! This "account rendered" scared me; I had not such a sum in my possession. Nothing daunted, however, I suggested that it should be put down in the school bill as "drawing materials." I was disappointed that my suggestion did not meet with approval. My governess pretended to be shocked at such a Machiavellian scheme. But as she was in a very sweet mood (the end of the term accounting for this, no doubt) I felt a little wheedling on my part would do no harm. Three minutes of this treatment proved so effective that it brought forth two excellent results. My fine was reduced to half, and my soft-hearted governess confessed that she considered I had not really deserved any more fines than some of the girls who only had to pay nine shillings for the whole term.

The reading of Massinger's play marked my introduction to the Elizabethan dramatists. When I reflected that Swinburne had embarked with intense enthusiasm on the study of the Elizabethan dramatic poets at the time of his early school days —or as he expressed it to me later, " when I was a kid at Eton"—and had pursued the study with ardour and energy ever since, it made me quite angry to think how I had been encouraged to read Racine and Molière, while the early English playwrights were known to me by name only.

Of course I could only suppose the French dramatists were *convenable* for the " English Meess," while the old English dramatists were not considered fit reading for the " young person." However, I started making up for lost time, and fortified by the perusal of Massinger's comedy, I felt I could now face Swinburne with more confidence, as I had at least made a start with the Elizabethans. A few days afterwards I met him on the door-step going out of the house on his walk to Wimbledon. Although I expected he had by this time forgotten all about me, I was agreeably surprised to find he had not done so.

I reminded him of his promise to show me his quartos. In awaiting his answer, I was not at all sure that he would remember having said anything about such a favour.

But he had not forgotten, and said he would be pleased to see me that very afternoon. For my part I looked forward to visiting him again with a very keen pleasure.

Swinburne's time for receiving visitors was always in the afternoon about four, so without his fixing the time, I knew I had to present myself at that hour.

There is many a slip between the cup and the lip, and I was astonished soon after lunch to receive this telegram from Walter :—" Postpone visit until to-morrow." The telegram was followed in the evening by a rather enigmatic lettter, telling me that Swinburne had changed his mind and preferred my going the next day, " as something he is giving you has not arrived, but is certain to be there if you will call at 4-30 to-morrow afternoon."

THE HOME LIFE OF SWINBURNE

Needless to say, I was full of curiosity, and arrived the next day long before the appointed time, bent on hearing all about it from Walter. Although I questioned him, as he declared, " like an Old Bailey barrister," I could get nothing out of him. My reiterated entreaties for enlightenment only produced repeated shakes of the head from left to right indicating " No," and the answer, " I promised Swinburne I would not tell you." Not another word on the subject could I drag from him. The longer I questioned him, the more decided became the head-shaking, and the merrier and more prolonged grew his chuckles. He seemed positively to enjoy my suspense. His remonstrance, " Now, Serjeant Ballantyne, don't you look at me like that " (as I gave him a final glance full of withering reproach), induced me to accept the inevitable and abandon any further attempts at cross-questioning. I had perforce to possess my soul in patience until I could learn the truth from the lips of Swinburne. I had not long to wait.

We had changed the subject and were talking of other things, when Swinburne himself appeared on the threshold. He came forward, and in a manner most cordial and gracious shook me warmly by the hand, and, signalling me to follow him, led

the way upstairs to his sanctum. Without any
preliminary talk, or explanation of the slightest
kind, he pointed to a neat little case of books on
the mantelpiece. Of course I was nonplussed.
Swinburne never uttered a word, but continued to
wave his hand towards the books without speaking
—unless the soft hilarious whistle he emitted, in
low staccato snatches, could be designated a form
of speech, and for a moment or two I did not know
what to say or do. But looking up for an instant
from the books to his face, I understood from his
dancing eyes and laughing expression the nature
of " the secret." He had anticipated my wishes
and procured from his bookseller at Wimbledon
the very fiction I said I wanted. The books
included two volumes of " The Adventures of
Sherlock Holmes," " Rodney Stone," " A Study
in Scarlet," and " The Sign of Four." Then it
appeared that Swinburne had made Walter
promise I should be kept in the dark until the
right moment came, and that he should be the
one to tell me that the non-arrival of the books at
the promised time was the reason of the postpone-
ment of my visit.

This little incident initiated me into Swinburne's
naïve and child-like methods of working out any
little scheme. Charming traits of character of this

kind were so frequently peeping out from him that it was difficult to think of him as the great poet whom all recognised as a King of Song. But it was only at first that it was puzzling, and before long I appreciated his boyish ways as characteristic of a personality which had all the transparency and poetic qualities of an elfin child who was at the same time a superlatively-gifted man.

The child-side of Swinburne appealed very strongly to Walter, who understood his curiously complex nature as did no other living being. I remember that once when, soon after his companion's death, I spoke of it to him, a far-away look of wistful tenderness came into his face. While the tears gathered in his eyes at the recollection, he turned to me and said:

"Dear Algernon, he was the simplest and noblest-minded creature in the world, by far the greatest poet, and one of the most lovable men I ever knew."

CHAPTER IV

SWINBURNE AS A BIBLIOPHILE

IT would be difficult to imagine a greater contrast between the idiosyncrasies of two men living under the same roof than that presented by the difference between Swinburne's tidy retreat upstairs and Walter's untidy workroom downstairs.

Coming direct from one into the other was positively startling, the difference being so marked as to suggest a sudden change from one country to another, such as genii could bring about in fairy tales.

I was conscious of a feeling of exaltation and repose in Swinburne's surroundings. The stillness and the tidiness had the quieting effect on the nerves that one feels on entering a cool cathedral on a hot day. The very aspect of the room breathed forth the spirit of its occupant's lofty purpose in life.

THE HOME LIFE OF SWINBURNE

Passionate book-lover that he was, he had arranged his treasures very carefully. Everything was in its place. At a first glance the room seemed to contain little besides books, but however much they might monopolise one's attention, it was impossible not to notice Swinburne's duster. It was so very obtrusive that you wondered why the back of a cane-seated Empire chair was chosen for the display of the red and yellow-checked affair which hung over it. But there it was, an object of undignified importance, gaily disporting itself almost in the middle of the room. I learned that it was one of the poet's little fads to have his own special duster always in sight, and easily got at whenever he had occasion to use it. And this was very often. He had a horror of even touching a dusty book, so, to be sure his library was kept in apple-pie order, he took the precaution of looking after his books himself. If he wanted to show you any particular book, he would first of all see that not a speck was on it. I can see him now, duster in hand, going carefully over the edges and cover to satisfy himself that all was as it should be before placing the volume in your hands. From that day, whenever I happened to enter his room, until the day he lay dying in this same room in which I now write these lines, I always saw

Swinburne's homely duster spread out in the funny way I have described.

The overflow of books which could not gain admittance to his shelves, found sanctuary on the wide sofa near the window, the same sofa on which Swinburne rested and sometimes slept in his Great James Street days.   It was an uncommonly long sofa, and filled more than half one side of the room not taken up by bookcases.   But at The Pines, in my time, he never used it to rest on ; it was reserved solely for the repose of books, which were piled high on it from end to end, not a square inch being available for a seat.

He would invariably sit on an easy chair with a circular back decorated with gold, the arms of which terminated in gold-covered rams' heads. There were two of these chairs in his study, and on the occasion of which I speak he pulled one out of a corner and invited me to sit on it, courteously remarking that he knew it to be comfortable.   He himself remained standing, hovering over the writing-table, with fluttering hands and breathing audibly in an excited way. And now, with a look absolutely radiating with pride of possession, he turned my attention to a bundle of very old and rather shabby-looking books.

THE HOME LIFE OF SWINBURNE

I knew these must be the precious quartos of first editions of the Dramatists, and when he took up one to inspect it before pointing out its manifold beauties to me, he uttered a rapturous "Ah!" as if he were looking at it for the first time and had discovered something new in it he had not noticed before. The handling of the volume seemed to afford him such delight that he could not refrain from making curious little sounds, as if his mouth were watering in anticipation of the succulent flavour of a peach. He was in no haste for me to inspect it, but turned to another and yet another volume over which he repeated the same performance, for all the world like a connoisseur, who in order to enjoy the full flavour of a wine, inhales the bouquet first. While the poet was inarticulately ecstasising, I was able to take a cursory glance at some of the volumes, in the hope that I might find a Massinger among them. I was becoming nervous at the rather long silence and wondered when Swinburne would break it.

How thankful I was I had a topic all ready, and could land on safe ground, and I began by telling him I had read "A New Way to Pay Old Debts." The news acted like a charm. I could not have hit upon a happier announcement, for, at the mere mention of this comedy, he became most animated, and his words poured forth like a torrent. He now brought forward his treasures with all the delight of a schoolboy showing his prizes.

With delicious *naïveté* he immediately jumped to the conclusion that I was an ardent student of the Elizabethan Dramatists. He took it for granted I had actually *read* all sorts of Elizabethan plays and shared his taste for them.

Poor Swinburne, child-like and simple in many ways, was especially so in this one. He could not conceive that one did not take his point of view about everything. Afterwards, when I saw him nearly every day and came to know him better, the mere mention by me of a book or a poem with which he was familiar and known to me perhaps only by name was quite sufficient for him to attribute to me a far greater knowledge of it than I actually possessed. I can't help smiling now when I think of it.

As he went on expatiating—his enthusiasm growing with every play to which he called my attention —I began to repent of my first rash admission. I know next to nothing of these Elizabethans or their plays, and not without difficulty could I have made out a line of the old-world type in which some of them were printed. With a rapt look he gazed upon this archaic typography, and as he tapped the page lovingly with his finger, he ejaculated, "Ah! Ah!" in a soft laughing tone as he raised his eyes to the ceiling. It was delightful to see him thus, but I felt instinctively the radiant look would at once vanish from his face if I told him that his idols were strangers to me. I had not the heart to disillusionise him, and I refrained from doing so.

Taking my courage in both hands I made an attempt to turn the discussion into another channel. My attempt did not meet with the success I thought it deserved. Swinburne looked at me with a shocked expression. What had aroused his indignation I did not discover till afterwards. Walter subsequently explained to me that if there was a thing in the world more than another that nettled the poet it was to have his conversation interrupted—especially if he happened to be holding forth on a favourite topic. On this occasion Swinburne's chivalry saved me from any spoken reproof, and I proceeded quite airily to talk about our friend Lady 'Archibald Campbell's production of " The Faithful Shepherdesse," in Coombe Wood, wherein she enacted the part of Perigot. But here again I was fated to upset the equanimity of my friend. I had alluded to the play as by " Beaumont and

Fletcher.'' The mention of the word Beaumont seemed to affect Swinburne as though one had offered him a personal insult. He glared, he shrugged his shoulders in a panic-stricken sort of way as one who despaired of the ignorance of the world. "Fletcher *only*!" he declared with tremendous emphasis. "Beaumont never wrote a line of it!" I dare not ask him how *I* was expected to know that; Beaumont and Fletcher were to me as inseparable as Marshall and Snelgrove or Darby and Joan.

It was curious to notice how a literary lapse of this kind roused Swinburne to fury. To me the point did not seem to matter much one way or the other. When betrayed into these little gusts of ill-temper in my presence, he was almost immediately penitent, and his contrition was as wonderful an expression of himself as had been his annoyance. After a while he began to talk quite amicably and reasonably about John Fletcher. He told me that when he went for his morning walk on the Common he always felt that Fletcher had once traversed the same spaces. He explained that Fletcher had lived for some time at Fulham Palace; that there was contemporary evidence to show that the dramatist had often walked about the Wimbledon stretches of woodland while staying at the Palace on the other side of the water, and that it was while wandering in Richmond Forest that he conceived the idea of " The Faithful Shepherdesse." " Ah ! " he added brightly " who knows but what the notion struck him as he passed by Lady Archie's delightful place ? "

This talk about Fletcher reminded me that some time previously I had attended a rehearsal by some enthusiastic amateurs of " The Two Noble Kinsmen." I waited until the poet had come to a full stop before venturing to mention this circumstance. Here at all events I had struck a sympathetic chord. His face lighted up wonderfully. He went over to the little mountain of books lying on the table.

" Ah ! " he exclaimed with childish delight, " I will read you something from ' The Two Noble Kinsmen.' "

But before the reading began a certain ritual had to be observed. The twilight was upon us. The poet lighted the three candles which always stood on his mantelpiece in three separate candlesticks. He hated gas as an illuminant though he was enthusiastic about the gas stove which was fixed in his bedroom fire-place—a contrivance he never attempted to light himself. Walter and I had often discussed the idea of installing electric light fittings to resemble candles. Perhaps he might have " taken to " the innovation. Perhaps not. In any case the idea was never carried out, and to the end of his days, when daylight began to fade, Swinburne read or wrote by the light of his three candles. His method of lighting was a fearsome process. On the landing outside his sitting-room door was an open gas-jet. He took one candlestick and lighted the candle at it, the grease dropping from it the while in unrestrained abandon. He returned to his room, the weapon in his hand still spluttering fat, and having placed the candle on the table, he lighted the other two from it. Then, with ceremonial precision, he arranged the three candles quite close together, almost touching each other. This light he kept behind him as he read. He seemed to know to a nicety the exact spot from which the light would be most effectively diffused, for the little circle of burning wicks afforded the sole illumination in his rather big study. While the soft rays from behind him were sufficient to make clear to him the printed page, they cast eerie shadows on the ceiling and threw wonderful high lights on the pictures and mirrors.

It struck me that many men, even poets, would have had either two or four candles in compliment to an unpleasant superstition by which three candles (possibly because there were three crosses at Calvary) are an omen of ill-luck. Whether or not Swinburne had ever thought of this superstition, the use of three candles was quite in keeping with his beliefs or misbeliefs.

But all my speculation about the superstition ceased when in mingled twilight and candlelight the poet began to read the passages in " The Two Noble Kinsmen " leading up to the fight between Palamon and Arcite.

There was a weird and subtle charm about Swinburne's delivery of the poetry that he loved. He had none of the arts or affectations of the elocutionist. There were indeed qualities in his method which the elocutionist would decry as unsound and eccentric. The fact, however, remains that his delivery captured the imagination of the hearer, where the art of the elocutionist left him cold. His methods may have been " unsound " · they were certainly effective. When I took leave of him after that memorable recital, it was with the sensation of one who had been hypnotised.

What, I wondered, made the Swinburne reading of an old dramatist so oddly arresting whereas his readings about Mrs. Gamp and others in the

Dickens gallery was so marred by peculiarities of voice and manner as to be almost unpleasant? With the qualities of the Dickens recitals I shall deal in a future chapter. The explanation is probably something like this : in Dickens he was most of all concerned with impersonation. He acted— or thought that he acted—the parts of the various characters. Nature had not endowed him with the equipment for accomplishing this ; so the performance left much to be desired. But when it came to giving voice to the words of an old dramatist he was no longer concerned with conveying the meaning to his audience. He surrendered himself completely to the rhythmic laws of verse. He rendered the music, not the meaning of the dramatist, and so it happened that while his rendering of Charles Dickens might be voted rather distressing, his reading of an act by John Fletcher arrested and fascinated the hearer.

CHAPTER V

SWINBURNE WHEN FIRST I KNEW HIM

EVEN when I knew Swinburne only by fleeting glimpses, the personality of the poet had struck me as something quite out of the ordinary.

To begin with, he looked what we call " a celebrity." Having once seen him, much less met him, no one could fail to understand he had come into contact with a very extraordinary being, for certain characteristics removed Swinburne definitely outside the pale of ordinary mortals. Had I met him for the first time in the street or in a room, and not knowing he was Swinburne, had been asked to guess what manner of man he was by profession, I should unhesitatingly at the first glance have said " Poet." A second guess might have been " Musician." This was not because he possessed the frenzied mane of hair which is such a valuable asset to a pianist, for

BUST OF A C SWINBURNE BY DRESSIER

when I first saw Swinburne his head was bald on top, his hair being a tawny-grey in colour. His face, however, reminded me of Paderewski. Both men possessed brilliant, expressive eyes, the same steady, intent gaze, and the same air of poetic mystery. Oddly enough, the hair on the temples and at the nape of the neck was rather thick, and was much ruddier than his other locks, indicating clearly that in his youth Swinburne had possessed red hair. His small beard and moustache, although streaked with grey, gave the same suggestion of warm colour.

Often when he sat opposite me at meals I would mentally frame Swinburne's head in the pianist's wealth of copper-coloured hair and the resemblance between them would then become positively surprising. But his hair had never been copper-coloured. When his cousin first showed me a lock of Algernon's hair, I could hardly believe such a colour could have grown on a human head. It was not a bit like the hair so often described as " the sort Titian would have loved to paint "; it was just a fiery red.

His eyes were what specially attracted me. They were wonderful, and by far the best feature of his face. If the eye is the window of the soul, truly the eyes of Swinburne spoke for him. I

would look at him long and searchingly across the
table to try to ascertain what colour they really
were. Sometimes they would look soft and tender
enough to suggest pansies, at other moments they
seemed to be greyish green; and, again, I would
think they must be blue. At last I came to the
conclusion that they were hazel. The peculiar
speckles in them made them marvellously
expressive. I have seen them dance and catch fire,
according to his various moods. When he read
aloud any passage requiring dramatic emphasis,
these speckles would grow more radiant and
quiver with every cadence of his rather high-
pitched voice.

Taking it for granted that Swinburne possessed
a superabundance of hair as a young man,
and wore it in the manner of " Struwwelpeter,"
I cannot agree with those who think that he
possessed a head too big for his body. I would
have been the first to have noticed any abnormality
of this sort, had it existed. In the days when his
figure was slender and boyish, the top-heavy look
with which he is credited was no doubt due to the
thick hair standing out bush-like from both sides
of his head.

Had Nature given Swinburne a body worthy of
his mental gifts, he would have been better looking

than the Āpollo Belvedere. But it was otherwise decreed. His facial features were remarkably good, but his figure was against him. He would have been handsome if he had been a few inches taller and his figure good. But he was short, and his shoulders were far too sloping.

His physical imperfections had become less noticeable when I knew him, for he had " filled out " since the days of " Dolores " and " Chastelard," and his limbs, unusually muscular, for a man of his size, had taken on a more solid look.

His hands were not beautiful or well-shaped, and they were not particularly small. I would often look at his rather podgy digits and prosaic finger nails, and compare them with Walter's long, tapering fingers and filbert-shaped nails. Walter's hand often served Rossetti for a model when the artist was painting one of his celebrated " half lengths," but one had to think of the work it did before one could be interested in Swinburne's hand. I feel called upon to make these observations because a brilliant essayist wrote in a leading review of Swinburne's hands and feet as though they were almost fairy-like.

À propos de bottes I had ample opportunity for knowing a good deal about the footwear of the

Housemates. The same bootmaker made for both of them. There was but little difference in size, Swinburne's feet being a trifle larger than Walter's. The poet took what in the trade is called " an eight and a half," so that to write of his " tiny feet " is absurd. Swinburne had his boots made of calf leather while Walter preferred a soft kid. Often when I was out walking with Walter I would notice that he had on a pair of calf boots. I would say, " You've got Swinburne's boots on again. Oh dear! Why will you not look? " Walter would laughingly reply, "And the joke of it is the poor boy can't get his feet into a pair of mine."

In the days of his young manhood, Swinburne may or may not have evinced a partiality for fine clothes, but I am sure his good sense never allowed him to adopt any sort of eccentricity of attire. The poet of tradition and the stage has always something of the guy about his clothing. He wears a pair of rusty black trousers, baggy at the knees, a nondescript waistcoat, and a shabby velveteen coat surmounted by a very low turned-down collar with a huge bow under it. His hair is long, and his hat is an umbrageous sombrero.

Swinburne's attire, as I observed it, flatly contradicted this caricature. He took great pains to avoid advertising his *métier*. He did not wear his hair long ; it only reached the nape of his neck, and the little he possessed was often cut by the barber.

He was always very plainly dressed, and I never saw him wearing any other sort of tie than a plain black silk one. At home, and sitting restfully in his chair with a book, he offered no mark for the caricaturist. But outside, when he had donned his wideawake, he somehow looked eccentric. For one thing he braced his trousers too high ; in his absence of mind, he would pull them above the ankles, showing several inches of white sock. Furthermore, he had a curious prancing gait, and his deliberate way of flinging out his feet before him as he trod the ground reminded one of a dancing-master or a soldier doing the goose-step.

With his head thrown stiffly back and his body almost rigid from the waist upwards, Swinburne out-of-doors seemed to me an individual distinct from the Swinburne at home. Owing perhaps to his deafness, he was averse from meeting even his friends out of doors. He hated to come across them suddenly, and even Walter or I, when we happened to meet him, refrained from taking the slightest notice of him as we passed. Often we would meet him face to face as he was coming

E   65

down or we were going up the Hill, or *vice versa.*
But he would walk past us totally oblivious of our
proximity. It certainly was not because he was
short-sighted, for he had perfect sight, but that
directly he had left the house his mind was ready
to take flight, like a bird on the wing, to that
sphere of inspiration, his beloved Common.

He would compose his poetry in the open air
as he walked along. On wending his way down
the Hill on his return, his thoughts were generally
far away in the world of music he had created, and
when he re-entered The Pines he was still thrilled
by the song he had been singing during his walk.

CHAPTER VI

THE HOUSEMATES

I HAVE never understood, and never expect
to understand, the motive actuating those persons
who, after the deaths of Swinburne and Watts-
Dunton, began to belittle the famous friends.
To me their intimacy is simple and beautiful.
The eyes of those who behold in it a
subject for ridicule or detraction must be the eyes
of the depraved. There is no chapter in literary
history dealing with men's friendship more lovely;
and yet envy and spite have tried to disfigure the
public aspect of this sweet and sacred thing.

I do not propose to relate *in extenso* the story
of how my husband and Swinburne came to live
together. That has been done accurately in
" The Life and Letters of Theodore Watts-
Dunton." The authors of that book had their
evidence at first hand. They heard the narrative

67

over and over again from Walter's own lips, just as I have heard it. They heard it from Mrs. Mason (Walter's sister), who received the poet at her own house when he first came to Putney with my husband. I have frequently heard the story from the same source. Mrs. Mason's narrative never differed on repetition, and that of Walter never differed circumstantially from that of his sister. I really cannot conceive of evidence more complete and convincing. Moreover, it is first-hand evidence given by those who had personal knowledge of the facts stated. Nevertheless, certain publicists found scope for misrepresentation, and the authentic story was met by printed expressions of doubt and denial.

The extraordinary thing is that Watts-Dunton's detractors deny statements made on first-hand testimony by quoting those made on third-hand evidence or no evidence at all. Perhaps I am only tempting these unscrupulous writers to fresh manifestations of spite by saying anything more about Swinburne's move to Putney, but I will take the risk. There is one pathetic passage in connection with the poet's first visit to Putney which was told me by Walter. It has not been published before. When Walter visited the sick poet, he was met by the landlady who, in answer to my husband's enquiry about the health of her lodger, said with an accent of deep concern :— " Well, sir, he haven't eat anything for days. A nice beefsteak 'ud do him a power o' good "; and when Walter went into his friend's bedroom, he felt that the first part of the lady's information must be true, whatever might be said for her dietetic suggestion in the second part of it. He looked terribly ill. When at length a visit to Putney as Walter's guest in his sister's house looked terribly ill. When at length a visit anxious eyes, and in a weak and broken voice asked eagerly, " Can't I go *now*? " It would have been quite impossible to have taken him then and there. But the hope of going, coupled with proper nourishment, worked a gradual change. When at last the patient was pronounced fit for the journey my husband appeared with the vehicle in which they were to travel. Swinburne was pitifully weak, and was obliged to have the assistance of Walter's arm in descending the stairs. He looked up at him with a flush on his pale cheeks and a wan smile on his lips. " Oh, I'm so glad I'm going to Putney with you," he said, in the manner of a boy who was going on a pleasure jaunt with a friend.

At Hyde Park Corner there was a congestion of

traffic. The carriage was held up in the block, and Lord Ronald Gower, who happened to be crossing the road at the time, saw who were the passengers in Walter's " growler." He went up to it and cried out, " Hullo, Watts, you've got Swinburne there. Where are you taking him to? " At that time Lord Ronald Gower did not know Swinburne, though naturally his appearance was well-known to one who moved, as Lord Ronald did, in literary and artistic circles.

Walter's reply to the enquiry was, " I'm taking him with me to Putney." Then the pedestrian proceeded to open the carriage-door exclaiming, " I'm coming, too." " Oh, no, you're not; we'll send you a card later on to say when you can come," was the prompt reply. As at that moment the tide of traffic began to flow again, the door of the " growler " was closed, and he went on his way rejoicing—which was also his way. Without any notion of doing an ill-natured thing (Lord Ronald was quite incapable of that) but from a pure love of fun, he started the rumour that Swinburne had been abducted by Theodore Watts, who had sternly refused him admittance to the conveyance in which he was carrying off his prey. I suppose the story never reached the ears of the housemates, as they became when they agreed to share the tenancy of The Pines. Lord Ronald duly received his invitation, and he and the poet immediately struck up a friendship which developed into a life-long intimacy. No visitor to The Pines was more welcome. Swinburne and this friend had much in common, and each delighted in the tastes and idiosyncrasies of the other.

Lord Ronald Gower was skilled in more arts than one. He was a sculptor, and he presented to Swinburne a bronze statuette of Victor Hugo, a really fine work which the poet valued, not only because it was a likeness of his Idol, but because it was the work of a friend. The statuette is in my possession, and a photographic reproduction of it appears in this book.

It was not, of course, until I became Walter's wife that I fully appreciated the exquisite nature of the relations existing between the two men. On Walter's side, the love for his friend seemed to be largely composed of what, for want of a better word, I must call the mothering instinct. He seemed to anticipate every wish and want of his companion. His anxiety for his physical welfare, his great interest in his mental output, his concern for his domestic comfort and for his amusement were beautiful to witness.

Swinburne's satisfaction in his domiciliary

arrangement with my husband can easily be understood. From his earliest correspondence it is obvious that he could rely but little on himself in the prosy affairs of the world. In his days of "roses and raptures" he found men who professed themselves willing to relieve him from tiresome responsibilities. But they turned out to be broken reeds—mere boon companions, or that less amiable class of individual with " axes to grind." In Walter he felt he had found the ideal friend upon whom he could rely, and his sentiment of gratitude and admiration soon developed into an indestructible brotherly affection. The infamous fiction, that my husband placed Swinburne under some kind of disciplinary restraint, would have been fiercely resented by Swinburne himself. Walter ruled him by love, guided him by advice, and influenced him by suggestion. With infinite patience and tact, he got him to change his habits, and it was not long before he discovered that he had by no means embarked on a hopeless task in trying to persuade his friend to lead the healthy, orderly life of which he was so much in need. It says much for Walter's magnetism that he was able to accomplish in a few months what the poet's medical man, his family, and other friends had given up as impossible.

THE HOUSEMATES

The author of "Atalanta" was just a human being who wanted to be loved and taken care of and directly he came to Mrs. Mason's house, under Walter's guidance, his cure began.

Those who have read Mr. Coulson Kernahan's clever narrative of the way in which Walter lured Swinburne from brandy to beer will remember the ingenuity displayed by my husband in bringing about the desired result.

I have often heard Walter tell the story, and veritably Swinburne's cure was effected by the art that conceals art. The Bard never detected that from first to last it was a ruse, for on the occasion of each change to a drink less potent than its predecessor, some literary reason was assigned which Walter guessed would awaken desire to emulate some real or fictitious hero beloved by Swinburne. As far as Algernon was concerned, he simply gave up brandy because Tennyson drank port, and changed from port to burgundy because that was the tipple of Dumas' immortal Musketeers. Then for an equally good reason he proceeded to claret, and, finally, as it was Shakespeare's drink, to beer.

Unfortunately, one day some time after my marriage Walter got it into his head that a very light beer, then extensively advertised and known as " Pilsener," would be quite the thing for Algernon and asked me to order some. Had he taken the precaution of informing Swinburne beforehand that this beer, he had reason to believe, was the established drink of, say, William Morris or Colonel Newcome, the Bard would have adopted it gleefully. But the bottle was placed before him one day at luncheon without any preliminary explanation. He poured it out quite unsuspectingly, and under the impression that it was his a̮customed " Ind Coope." Having tasted it, however, he flatly refused to drink the " stuff," and with an angry glint in his eyes he peremptorily ordered the maid to bring his usual drink to him.

Nothing shows more effectively the success of Walter's influence over Swinburne's early failing than the fact that when he took his daily walks across the Common to Wimbledon, he was perfectly free to indulge in whatever beverage he chose, but was never known to exceed his one bottle of beer at his favourite inn.

I think I shall best indicate the attitude of the housemates each to the other by quoting what on two different occasions was said to me. Swinburne old me one day, with an expression of infinite tenderness in his eyes : " There is no one in the

A C SWINBURNE AND T WATTS DUNTON IN THE GARDEN OF
THE PINES

world like Walter!" By the way, he never called him Theodore as he is made to do by one writer of reminiscences.

My husband said to me long before that tribute was paid him by Swinburne, " It is because of his helplessness that I love him so much." No words of mine can more adequately than these depict the sweet relationship existing between the men, its quality and its cause, the unceasing and ungrudging tenderness of the protector, the unfailing and unfaltering gratitude of his friend and housemate.

But prejudice and malice can make critics view life through a distorting glass. Only this can account for the fact that when Swinburne was rescued from pitiable surroundings and mischievous companionship, and placed in comfortable quarters, the cry went round that the physical improvement of the poet synchronised with his mental decay. So highly placed was the originator of the legend, and so impartial and judicial appeared to be his tone, that it was repeated by the smaller fry of critics, and accepted by the denser sort of readers.

The opponents of the change wrought by my husband in Swinburne's manner of living are fond of asserting that his verse deteriorated in quality after he left Great James Street. Apparently they deplore the cessation of the moods to which we owe " Faustine," " Dolores," or " Hermaphroditus." They fail to appreciate the fact—or, appreciating it, they disingenuously refrain from stating it—that a continuous supply of bitterly erotic verse from the same source would eventually have palled upon the public. We are invited to suppose, however, that there are critics who would never sicken of repetitions of the first series of " Poems and Ballads," and when the poet leaves his *grandes amoureuses* and lepers, then —oh, most amusing paradox!—they dub him decadent.

I turn for relief from the raucous chorus of detractors to the verdict of Mrs. Disney Leith, whose capacity for judging was not diminished by her cousinship with the poet. She has written of his career with discernment and comprehension :—" The time of his vivid and fiery youth was not that of his best production. It was in the little home at Putney, with its quiet household routine .   .   .   that the great imperishable works of his life were brought forth." In support of this statement, I surrender to the temptation of quoting what from a technical tandpoint is one of the best sonnets ever written, that which Swinburne addressed to Walter after they had spent two years together at The Pines:

Spring speaks again, and all our woods are stirred
   And all our wide glad wastes aflower around,
   That twice have heard keen April's clarion sound
Since here we first together saw and heard
Spring's light reverberate and reiterate word
   Shine forth and speak in season. Life stands crowned
   Here with the best one thing it ever found
As of my soul's best birthdays dawns a third.

There is a friend that as the wise man saith
   Cleaves closer than a brother: nor to me
   Hath time not shown, through days like waves at strife,
This truth more sure than all things else but death,
   This pearl most perfect found in all the sea
   That washes toward your feet these waifs of life.

I dismiss an unpleasant subject by saying that the argument against those who belittle Swinburne's later work needs no exponent except the " waifs of life " to be found in " Studies in Song," " Tristram of Lyonesse," and the volumes which followed them.

CHAPTER VII

THE HAWTHORNS

In his wanderings over Wimbledon Common and Putney Heath, Swinburne cultivated the acquaintance of trees as other men cultivate the acquaintance of their fellow-creatures. His prime favourites were the Hawthorns. When the May was in full blossom the poet's enthusiasm was wonderful to witness. He never tired of talking about the beauty of these sweet-smelling bushes. His endeavour after one of his rambles seemed to be to inspire us with an enthusiasm equal to his own.

Swinburne's interest in trees dated from his early experiences of Northumberland. He often declared that the scenery of his beloved County was wilder and more magnificent than any other in England. He knew the name of a tree the moment he saw it. No chance of the Bard mistaking an elm for an oak, or a beech for a birch. And the difference between particular members of the same sylvan species was to him as distinct as the difference between one man and another. Many of the trees he knew by the familiar names bestowed upon them by the rustics of Northumberland. His lore concerning trysting oaks and white poplars, about an old ash or a silver fir, was quite interesting, and apparently inexhaustible. I was always prepared to listen sympathetically to his eloquent tributes to his sylvan favourites, but I confess I was not prepared for the proposition he made to me one day on this subject.

" When," he asked, without any prefatory leading up to the topic—" When are you coming with me to see the hawthorns? "

I was thinking of something quite different at the time, and for just a moment his question sounded as if he indicated an afternoon call on a family of that name. A recollection, however, of certain of his rhapsodies over the luncheon-table made the illusion a momentary one. The Hawthorns to whom he was anxious to introduce me were arboreal friends of his, and not mere creatures of flesh and blood. Nothing definite was settled at the time of this first invitation. Swinburne reverted to it almost daily.

On one occasion his tone had a pathetic and pleading note in it. " Don't let us wait until the blossoms are falling," he urged. " When are we going to see the May? " Both Walter and I felt that the expedition could no longer be put off. A day and hour were settled. We arranged to meet the poet on Putney Heath close to the house of the late Sir George Newnes. It turned out to be an ideal day when my husband and I started off to keep our appointment, which to me seemed a great adventure, for I had been but six months married, and still felt romantically the novelty of my position.

When we arrived at the trysting-place, we found Swinburne already there pacing up and down, watch in hand, in a state of great impatience. We were, as our American friends put it, " on time," if, indeed, we were not more than punctual. But the poet had evidently been experiencing considerable nervousness and anxiety. He would not imagine us forgetful, but he had conjured up some unforeseen and unfortunate circumstance preventing us from keeping our appointment. His relief at our arrival was great, and he was for darting off on the instant to introduce us to the " hives of the honey of heaven " which at this spot were particularly luxuriant. Walter, however, had a business appointment at home and he left us together. I strolled off with Swinburne. I found that he knew each one separately and individually, as one knows old friends. He ran from one to another, jumping over the numerous intersecting dykes and ditches and giving me his hand to help me to leap over to his side. When he got to one large hawthorn of divine loveliness he paused for a long time in front of it and drew in long deep breaths, as though he were inhaling the subtle emanation of the blossoms he so rapturously adored, and softly and repeatedly ejaculated, "Ah-h-h!" In front of another hawthorn, exceptionally tall and weighed down with " the marvel of May time," he said, " This is one I especially want you to see. Of course it is rather too big for a hawthorn." With this expression of opinion I thought he dismissed the tree, but his respect for it was greater than his disapproval of its dimensions would have led me to expect. Before he turned to leave, he took off his hat, and gravely saluted the big beauty of the hawthorn tribe.

A little further on he said to me, " Now I will show you one quite different—much smaller." After some quick walking and occasional jumping of ditches, he halted me in front of a short, stumpy and very bushy tree perfectly white in its mantle of blossom. He gazed at it with the idolatrous affection of a lover. Then he turned to me, and asked with a sort of chastened enthusiasm, " Now, is not *that* a little duck? " " Duck," I may add, was a favourite word of the Bard's when alluding to little things that he loved. I thought it strange at the time that he did not appear to take any great interest in the other glories of the heath— the yellowing gorse, the ferns just showing their fronds, the heather with its fascinating odour. He was subconsciously aware of them, of course, but his visit—and mine—was to the Hawthorns, and for the time being, the other beauties of the heath did not count.

Looking back on it now, I don't know which of us enjoyed that " hawthorn time " the more, or which of us was the younger of the two. I think it must have been Swinburne. He was absolutely indefatigable. All this jumping about in the broiling sun in the hottest part of the day did not affect him in the least, whereas it left me decidedly limp. I was struck with his agility, it resembled that of some free animal of the wood-lands. He repeated as we moved on, and apparently to himself, without any thought of having a hearer, the lines :

THE HAWTHORNS

In hawthorn time the heart grows light,
The world is sweet in sound and sight.

But the hearer on this occasion recognised the quotation. " Why," I said to him " those are the opening lines of ' The Tale of Balen '!" He stopped short in his stride, his expression one of combined surprise and pleasure. " Have *you* read ' The Tale of Balen '? " he asked. I told him for the second time—for he had completely forgotten about the talk at our first meeting—that not only had I read " Balen," but that Walter had asked me to transcribe it, and that I knew every word of it. He seemed greatly interested in my statement and gave me a look like an unspoken benediction.

Swinburne abominated typewriting, and latterly all his poetry was copied by hand before it went to the printers who set up from copy while the original remained in the poet's possession. I remember how the Bard would snatch up his proofs as soon as they arrived " to see what the devils were up to "—meaning the compositors. Here I may say that Swinburne's usual practice was to publish everything he wrote directly he was satisfied with it. Walter said to me, "Algernon is the exact opposite to me. I am loth to publish anything. Swinburne burns to see his work in proof."

But to return to our walk. Swinburne's talk as we gained the road was mainly about the gorgeous sights and delicious odours from which we had just emerged. But these did not provide the whole of his subject matter. I happened to mention the name of a man of whom—from the expression that his countenance suddenly assumed —he evidently did not approve. The poet stopped and growled out a word which I could not catch. It sounded like " Polly " something, and I supposed my friend wished to convey the idea of effeminacy in the gentleman whose name I had mentioned. Some time after I asked him to tell me what word he had used. He was in one of his most amiable moods, and he not only repeated the word but he wrote it down for me in very large and distinct letters. I have still preserved it as a memento. Here it is :

" polypseudonymuncle."

Asked about its precise meaning, he readily answered that it meant " a horrible little sewer-rat who had been convicted under a hundred aliases " I expressed my surprise that one word could convey so many. He declared that he quite shared my feeling. 'As we were nearly home, and about to cross the road, a pony-cart passed up the hill. The cargo of the driver consisted of caged birds. It was a miscellaneous lot. It appeared to comprise all sorts and conditions of bird from the canary to the cockatoo. Prominent among the captives were some parrots, and I drew the poet's attention to a depressed specimen crouching at the end of his perch in a cage far too small for him. Some association of ideas set the poet off on a fresh conversational track. He asked me if I had ever heard of a wonderful parrot at one time in the possession of his sister. I shook my head. He proceeded to expatiate on the recorded exploits of the gaudy and gifted creature His sister's parrot—so he said he had been assured— both sang and recited " *Malbrouck s'en va-t'en guerre* " with the utmost fluency. " Did he swear? " I enquired. "Alas! No," said Swinburne. " Although he had been adopted by a naval family, the creature was innately genteel and Victorian.''

After a silence he resumed his reminiscences. He told me that one day Walter and he had gone to lunch with his sister Alice. With a mock tragic air he explained that it was a sad occasion.

THE HOME LIFE OF SWINBURNE

The feathered pet had, in a tolerably green old age, paid the debt of nature. His sister was naturally much distressed at the loss of her bird. And Alice being the Bard's favourite sister, he was naturally affected by the depression of his hostess. The meal was a dull affair, and on leaving the house Swinburne again and again expressed his regret that anything should have happened to have upset her so gravely. " But," said Swinburne, " my one regret was that my deafness never allowed me to hear the talented creature sing his famous little French song. How I should have enjoyed that ! "

I would dearly have liked to continue our walk, for Swinburne's ebullient spirits were contagious and he was in a particularly lively mood. But the luncheon-hour was approaching, and we were obliged to turn our backs to the country and make tracks for home. He appeared charmed when I told him how much I had enjoyed seeing the Hawthorns, and of my wish to pay them another visit. He beamed with pleasure at the idea of being again my " cicerone," as he called it, and immediately suggested that his sister Isabel should join our next expedition. " I'll write to her this afternoon," he said, " and urge her to come."

I used to love the days when Isabel came to

The Pines. To see the brother and sister greet each other was a positive delight, such simple and devoted affection did the one entertain for the other.

On reaching home, Swinburne followed me into the room where Walter sat waiting for us. Full of animation, the poet said, " Clara and I have seen my beautiful Hawthorns ; and it was like being with a hamadryad—absolutely a hamadryad.

The letter to Isabel was duly despatched and both Swinburne and I looked forward to showing her " the little duck " and all the other wonders of the heath. Alas ! on the day she elected to come it poured with rain, and the visit had to be put off until a more propitious occasion. Swinburne was as disappointed as a child.

CHAPTER VIII

Now that Damon and Pythias have passed " beyond the veil," I think of the gentle, affectionate and always courteous attitude of Swinburne towards myself. I was admitted as a privileged member of the inner circle. On my part I did all in my power to make myself acquainted with the literary topics they discussed, and trained myself to take an intelligent interest in their conversation, which often, I quite freely admit, was miles above my head. Swinburne, when first informed that Walter and I were to be married, expressed himself very characteristically. " You know," he said to Walter, " I think all this is very jolly." He took unusual pains in the selection of a wedding-present for us, which on this occasion did not take the shape of books. Something different had to be thought of, and he had set his mind on "something beautiful in silver." He applied to his sister Isabel to aid him in his quest. He eventually selected an exquisite dish in dull beaten silver, the signs of the Zodiac in coloured enamels embellishing its artistic column and base. I recall too that when our marriage was announced he and Walter went off at once to Onslow Square to convey what the poet described as " the wonderful news " to his sister. Then he became impatient in his desire to make me acquainted with her. Miss Isabel Swinburne was the last surviving member of the poet's family and the youngest of his four sisters, none of whom married, his younger brother Edward being the only one of Admiral and Lady Jane Swinburne's children to quit the single state. When I saw Isabel for the first time she was about fifty-four years of age. She was still very good-looking, and as a girl must have been extremely pretty. She was of medium height, inclined perhaps to be a trifle stout, her complexion was creamy in its smooth excellence, her eyes angelically blue. Her movements had the agility of youth. Elegance and refinement united in her with *esprit* and subtle charm. Some might have called her gushing, but in her case an effusion of pleasant words implied to me sympathy and tenderness. Moreover, she easily saw the funny side of things. Swinburne invariably addressed her as "Abbas," a nursery name. To her and a few close friends he was " Hadji."

Walter accompanied me on my first visit to Isabel Swinburne. The reception she gave me was delightfully cordial and obviously sincere, and we soon became great friends. She at once insisted on my calling her " Isabel," and when I forgot this friendly injunction, she reminded me of it by saying, in her inimitably pretty way, that she did not know who " Miss Swinburne " was. As to Swinburne's attitude of brotherly affection to myself, he took an early opportunity of assuring me that he looked upon me as " something near." In proof of this declaration he presented me with a beautiful edition of " Lorna Doone " bound in white vellum, with this inscription :

> To Clara Watts-Dunton,
>   From her affectionate brother-in-law
>   Algernon Charles Swinburne.

The gift afforded me unbounded pleasure, and the inscription seemed to assure me that the fraternal bond that held the two housemates was undisturbed by my coming. The sumptuous volume was illustrated with thirty-seven landscape views of the scenery round and about the Doone Valley. I well remember how, on the day he gave it to me, he enthusiastically cut open the pages facing the illustrations and drew my attention to a particularly lovely one depicting Porlock Bay. He gazed on it for a long time, declaring it to be worthy of Turner, whom he considered the greatest landscape painter in the world.* But when we came across a full-page illustration of three human figures he hurried past it with an unmistakable sign of annoyance, and confided to me that he hated (Swinburne never disliked anything— he always hated or loathed it) illustrated books where human beings were portrayed. He told me that one of his reasons for choosing that particular edition was because he imagined it to be free from such pictorial eyesores. Nothing in a small way vexed him more than to find, even in a magazine, an illustration to a story with a footline of this sort :—" Suddenly, she looked him

---

* Turner gave Swinburne's mother, Lady Jane Swinburne, six original water-colour drawings. She treasured them so much that she would never go anywhere without them. Whenever the family travelled abroad, a portfolio containing the precious drawings always accompanied them. I was privileged to see them on more than one occasion. They were unframed, and kept in the portfolio always, and never allowed to be exposed, in case the light should fade their wonderful colour.

straight in the face." My imagination refuses to conjure up what he would have said if he had seen the portrait of himself as a hairy Satyr delighting an audience of naked babes, which adorns the posthumous collection of his child-poetry entitled " The Spring-tide of Life."

CHAPTER IX

SWINBURNE'S CONSTITUTIONAL

SWINBURNE'S daily walk across the Common to Wimbledon and back has been done to death. Every yard of the way has been described; and, indeed stretches of the heath which were not included in his itinerary have been " written up " and photographed. Imaginative writers have boldly identified his favourite spots. But these enthusiasts have, as a rule, ended their narratives at the very point where cynics might suppose the human interest of the story to begin, namely, the village of Wimbledon itself. For the limit of Swinburne's walk was the old-fashioned inn known as " The Rose and Crown." Elsewhere I have described one of my walks with the poet over his beloved common, with the remarks he made to me on his favourite trees. Here I follow him to his favourite inn, and to the shop at which he bought a daily paper and sometimes ordered, from a catalogue, some rare old book which the owner of the shop would procure for him. At both the inn and the shop Swinburne's memory is still cherished with affectionate reverence.

Visitors will find the exterior of " The Rose and Crown " exactly as it was in the poet's day. The interior has, alas! been altered out of recognition. I shudder to think what the effect on Swinburne would have been had the architectural transformation been effected in his time. The cosy little " coffee room " which he entered from the street has disappeared, and with it has disappeared the chair in which he always sat. But it is in safe keeping; and I just loved the widow of the late landlord when she told me that she would not part with it for any sum that might be offered

When once Swinburne had established himself as a daily customer at " The Rose and Crown " he was spared the usual formality of ordering. From the bar his entry was noted. They had been keeping a look-out for him, and a waiter entered from without " bearing a bottle of Bass with a replica of the peculiarly thick tumbler which the Bard used at home. It is related, with a note of tragedy in the recital, how this sacred beaker, which was kept for his use, was smashed by a careless barmaid. Unfortunately there was not another such glass in the house. Swinburne was greatly " put out " by the accident. He did not relish his Bass from any other vessel; was moody and silent during his stay, leaving the place abruptly after but a very short rest. Happily, on the same afternoon a stock of tumblers like that which had been broken was procured, and from the morrow until the end the poet was provided with the vessel that he preferred.

The cosy little apartment which he used was not much frequented during the time of his visit; but it was not, of course, a private room, and a stray visitor would sometimes enter it while the poet was in possession. Then one of two things happened. If Swinburne had nearly finished his bottle, he would get up and disappear into the village High Street. If, on the other hand, he had only just begun to refresh himself, he would seek sanctuary in the landlord's private room. As all his movements were watched by the host or his assistants with a really pious solicitude, he would immediately be followed to his retreat by a servant bringing with him the bottle and the glass which the poet had abandoned in the " Coffee Room." It is as well to say here that

THE HOME LIFE OF SWINBURNE

Swinburne's intense love of privacy has given rise to a vast amount of foolish and sometimes spiteful talk about his inaccessibility at The Pines. He was not inaccessible to those he desired to see.

I have often thought when viewing Swinburne's life at The Pines both before and after my marriage, that Sydney Smith may have been quite wrong in ridiculing the idea of a " Special Providence." For surely some unseen power must have arranged matters for the convenience of the Bard. When he made his first excursions to Wimbledon he at once discovered the very people who seemed intuitively to understand how he wished to be served. These admirable persons may have been entertaining an angel. But they were not entertaining the angel " unawares." As we have seen, he daily found at an Inn (the first and only one he went to at Wimbledon) a host and hostess who might have been appointed by the Almighty to minister to his needs after the very fashion he desired.

A little higher up the village High Street he came, during his first exploratory ramble, on the shop of a bookseller and stationer. Here he

established himself on an excellent footing with
the proprietress, and here, for thirty years, he
repaired every week day of his life while he was
living at Putney to buy newspapers. Books he
also bought here, and, in December, Christmas
cards. Of his Christmas cards I shall have something to say elsewhere.

When the poet returned from his daily walk,
buoyant, excited and invigorated by the exercise,
the conversation at lunch often turned on the
Wimbledon book-shop and its amiable owner, Miss
Frost. Swinburne imagined that he had
discovered in her a survival of the gentle, placid,
efficient Englishwoman limned in the pages of
Jane Austin. Miss Frost knew the identity of her
illustrious customer, and was especially anxious to
make things pleasant for him. She succeeded
marvellously, and Swinburne was quite at ease in
her establishment.

There is a class of hero-worshippers who would
intrude on the privacy of an eremite for the sake
of telling their friends that they had interviewed
" a celebrity." Wimbledon had its proportion
of this unpleasant and persistent tribe; and
it would happen sometimes that Swinburne was
tracked down by one of these persons. The
hunter was usually, I am sorry to say, a woman.

She would come in, and under the pretence of purchasing a " H.B." pencil or a pennyworth of blotting-paper, endeavour to force herself upon the notice of the poet. Miss Frost was prepared for such emergencies, and if the obtrusive " Mrs. Leo Hunter " were not forced to a retreat by the great man's freezing glance, he would escape molestation by withdrawing to the private room of the sympathetic bookseller. It must be admitted that A. C. S was in the habit of accepting considerate attention of this kind too much as a matter of course. But that he was *au fond* grateful and appreciative I have the very best authority for stating.

On one occasion an aggressive lady, blessed with one of those voices that are said to " carry," actually went up to the poet and expressed a desire to shake hands with him. He glared, irresponsive. She repeated the request, raising her voice to the whole extent of its carrying power. He made a characteristic movement of the shoulders indicative of deafness and despair, and rushed out of the shop. On the following day when he paid his visit to his bookseller, he exclaimed abruptly to Miss Frost : " What a terrible woman that was yesterday ! And oh, what an awful voice ! " He had evidently heard the request of the huntress. The voice had " carried " all right.

Very curious I thought this desire on the part of people who did not know Swinburne—and of some who did not even know his works—to shake hands with him. When I went into society, enthusiastic persons with whom my acquaintance was of the thinnest possible kind would come up and say: " Oh, Mrs. Watts-Dunton, *could* you arrange for my son (or nephew or daughter as the case might be) to call at The Pines just to shake Mr. Swinburne by the hand." To these I would say: " I will ask Mr. Swinburne and let you know." Of course I never spoke to the poet of these hand-shaking sentimentalists, for he simply loathed their sort of homage and was extremely sensitive on the subject.

Swinburne had a horror of drawing small cheques. Only with difficulty could he be persuaded to draw one for five pounds; below that he absolutely refused to go. Periodically he got the bookseller at Wimbledon to change him a cheque for twenty pounds. The money was obtained in gold from the bank at the other side of the street. He took it away in the little canvas bag used by bankers, and this bag, when he returned to The Pines was placed on a shelf in the corner cupboard where he kept his manuscripts. The bag was always open, and so was the cupboard. From this store of gold he drew for his daily requirements until the little bag was empty. Then he would draw another cheque for twenty and get Miss Frost to cash it. For a long series of years, indeed, this lady played the part of a fairy godmother to him. And it is not everybody, I can assure the reader, who is qualified to play fairy godmother to a genius.

Sometimes the Wimbledon purchases grew to a considerable bulk. Swinburne in a bookseller's was something like a schoolboy in a tuck-shop. Temptation was on all sides of him, and he found it irresistible. For the carriage of his treasures he had two very large pockets in his coat. We called them his " poacher-pockets." One of the self-imposed duties of the kindly bookseller at Wimbledon was to see that these poacher-pockets balanced nicely. The poet himself was not deft in stowing away his purchases; and with one heavy pocket weighing down on one side and a light one on the other, the walk home across the Common would have been fatiguing even to such an excellent pedestrian.

I can fancy him now, impatient but tractable, as

he stands while the adjustment of the parcels is proceeded with, his relief when the balance is decided to be " just so," his courtly bow on departure and his quick, springy walk home across the Common. 'And I can see him now as, on his return, he comes into the dining-room, gay and beaming and, to my thinking, beautiful. His eyes would sparkle with sheer delight as he produced some of the morning's " finds." Perhaps it was a rare old volume ordered long since from a catalogue. Perhaps some freakishly small edition of a classic. Dwarf reproductions afforded him infinite pleasure. Perhaps it was a newspaper containing a complimentary notice of some work by a friend, or a notice, equally laudatory, of a writer whose output he despised. The latter he would read in impressive tones, exclaiming at the finish, with a roguish twinkle in his eyes, " I should much like to feel that person's ' bumps.' " This phrenological phrase was often used by him when referring to somebody who, in the direction of bad art, might be regarded as *capable de tout*.

During luncheon he would talk brightly, vividly, and at times eloquently, of books and men. With a courtliness which was one of his most delightful characteristics, he would lure me into the conversation, amusing me with gossip about what he saw on Wimbledon Common and ask when I next would accompany him on one of his walks. The world will always—and rightly—honour him as a great poet. To me he appealed also as a great gentleman.

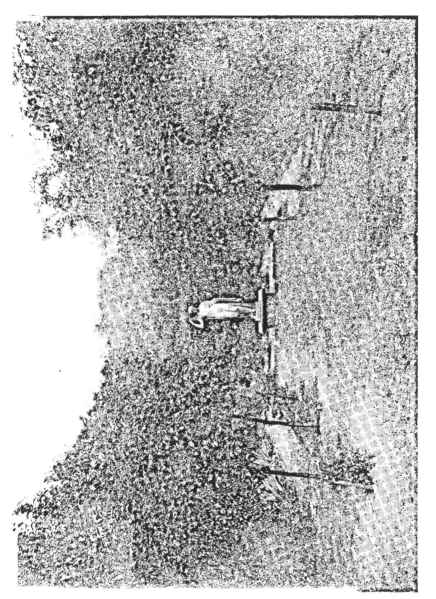

THE GARDEN OF THE PINES FROM THE WINDOW OF SWINBURNE'S STUDY

THE STATUE, A COPY OF THE VATICAN VENUS, CAME FROM ROSSETTI'S GARDEN

CHAPTER X

A POET'S FADS

I BEGIN writing this chapter in that upstairs room at The Pines once known as " Swinburne's Library." From the window in front of which I am sitting, the garden on which the poet's eyes so often rested, is in full view. He loved it. Its green refreshed his eyes after poring over his books or working at his manuscript. Spring was a season that always appealed to him. The garden then was a solace and delight. It is Spring now, and the picture has not changed. The high ivy-clad walls, the huge ferns beneath, which came from my husband's home at St. Ives, and the tall trees in the background all look as delightfully verdant as they did in Springs when he was on earth.

Floriculture was not a hobby with either of the housemates. There are masses of purple iris on either side of the stretch of grass, and we boasted of one rose-tree. It bears the fascinating name of " Hebe's Lips," and was given to me by Lady Leighton-Warren. I planted it by the statue that stands in the middle of the enclosure—a replica of the Vatican Venus, moved from Rossetti's garden at 16, Cheyne Walk, Chelsea, to its present position. A thrush is singing somewhere in the fringe of foliage. From the outer world comes the hoot of a motor-horn and the rumble of heavy traffic. In my loneliness the past comes vividly back to me. And here, in this room—dedicated to the greatest poet of the Victorian period—recollections drive on me in waves; my memory is suddenly like a stream in spate. And the difficulty with me is what to select as memorable and what to reject as trivial.

Yet can anything that concerns the home life of a poet like Swinburne—a genius so universally acclaimed—be dismissed as trivial? I hope not. For here, in the room that was once his, the memories that crowd in upon me are not those of the maker of glorious song, but those associated with the affectionate friend, the lovable companion. His greatness does not concern me. My recollections are all of his little personal traits, his delightful idiosyncrasies, his fads and fancies—a phase of the poet's personality unknown to the outside world. It is of this aspect of Swinburne that I now write, sitting where he often sat, and wondering if he has discovered whether

> His life is a watch or a vision
> Between a sleep and a sleep.

Swinburne had no end of " fads." It was a whim of his, for instance, never to allow himself to be measured or fitted by a tailor. There must have been an occasion, of course, and that, too, when he had grown to manhood, when he was obliged to submit to the indignity. And I can imagine his restlessness and irritability when the tape was thrown over and around his person, when chalk marks were made on the " fittings," and when plebeian hands patted his shoulders and fussed over his limbs. But there came a time when he declared he would no longer endure the ordeal. And he never again did. If he wanted a new suit, it had to be made on the model of an old one. The tailor always protested · " I cannot do myself justice," he would say. Whereupon A. C. S. would consign all tailors to fire and brimstone— to everlasting disaster in this world and to eternal damnation in the world to come. The affair would be happily arranged, and the result quite wonderful. The clothes were always an admirable fit, and though it was impossible for Swinburne to wear clothes to the best advantage, he always appeared well-dressed. From my woman's point of view, the extraordinary circumstance is that the tailor working under such harassing conditions was able to show such good results.

Another curious fancy of Swinburne's was about soap. He had discovered—or a friend had discovered for him—a brand known as " Samphire Soap," which was extensively advertised by a quotation from " King Lear " ·

> Half way down
> Hangs one that gathers samphire, dreadful trade!

This precious tablet smelt of the sea. Or was supposed to smell of the sea. A. C. S. believed implicitly that it was highly charged with the active principle of ozone. He sensed the wave in its odour, and the suds in his bath were refreshing to him as the foam of the ocean. Needless to say, " Samphire " soap was a thing of which we never permitted ourselves to " run short " I still keep a cake of it as a souvenir of the happiest time of my life.

Swinburne seemed constitutionally averse from doing anything himself which he could get others to do for him. For instance, he refused absolutely to open himself any letters addressed to him except those from members of his family. This duty was supposed to devolve on Walter. But very often it became mine. The handwriting and post-marks sufficiently indicated the family letters, which were given to the Bard unopened. The others were what one would expect—letters from admirers, from publishers, from " friends," and a great number from autograph-hunters. With appeals of the last-named the poet's post-bag was always well supplied—" full measure and running over." Most of these applicants were unknown persons having no claim whatever on the amiability of the poet. Their missives were consigned to the waste-paper basket. We had a printed form which we sent to a selected few In this Mr. Swinburne " presented his compli-ments " to the writer and regretted that he " was obliged to make it a rule not to supply his autograph. Some of the applicants resented this polite refusal. But what was one to do? Anyhow, it was comparatively easy to deal with this class of correspondent; but Swinburne's disinclination to open his letters once had embarrassing conse-quences for me.

My husband had handed me a batch of letters which from their covers appeared to be of the usual circular sort, or of the autograph-hunting variety, and I proceeded to open them mechanically. Then I came to a politely-worded letter from Lord Curzon to the poet. This, I at once felt, placed itself in the same category as communications from the family—a missive which should have been opened only by A. C. S. himself. 'At once I jumped up and ran with it to Walter. Although my husband never in his life said an unkind word to me, I judged from his expression that he was greatly annoyed and distressed. He desired me to go to Swinburne myself and explain the matter. I went. I anticipated some irritation on the part of the addressee of the note—perhaps words of rebuke and reproach. Nothing of the kind happened. He took the letter from me, read it, smiled at my expressions of apology and regret, and declared in his urbane way, " I am so sorry you should feel troubled over so trifling a thing. I will answer the letter myself after I have shown it to Walter." Days elapsed before the answer was written. He came into our room with it and handed it to my husband. " Do you think this will do? " he asked. No one could have guessed from his casual manner that the letter was of any particular importance. It was, however, his reply to Lord Curzon delicately but definitely declining the honorary degree offered by his old University of Oxford.

Swinburne's preference for a large foolscap paper of an unusually deep blue will be recollected by those who have seen his **MSS.** Ream upon ream of this stationery must have been used up during the years of his life passed at The Pines. It was as permanent a household requirement as the " Samphire " soap. Perhaps, like that toilet requisite, it reminded him of the sea.

No doubt the reader will find it hard to visualise the poet as a leader of fashion. Nevertheless, it has to be recorded that in one article of attire he set the mode. He was the pioneer of the starchless collar and soft-fronted shirt, for he wore them years before I was born. In the period to which he always referred as " when I was a kid at Eton," he had stiffness enough in his linen to last him a lifetime. Freed from the tyranny of the Eton " house " laundress, he forswore starch and had the courage to sacrifice glossiness for comfort. It is something to have lived to see unstarched body-linen become as popular as the " Poems and Ballads."

Fancies ought not to be confounded with fads,

but they have a sort of cousinship with them and are not altogether inappropriate to this chapter. Let me therefore say something here about Swinburne's taste in newspapers.

Lord Burnham may be interested to learn that Swinburne's morning paper was the *Daily Telegraph*. The Bard had no sympathy whatever for Matthew Arnold's fine disdain for this organ ; he attributed it to jealousy. Arnold— he told my husband—was wroth because the *Daily Telegraph* was edited for years " by a fellow of the same name." He would maliciously add " and I understand that both these journalists employ their moments of leisure in writing verses " The *Telegraph* appealed to him as a youth. " There is too much *We*-ishness about *The Times*," I once heard him say, the allusion being of course to the stately editorial " We " of the leading article. On another occasion a friend quoted to him a *Times* article in which the " We " of Printing House Square administered a solemn warning to a certain foreign power. " It reminds me," said Swinburne, " of an editorial article in an Irish paper called the *Skibbereen Eagle*. The article began, " We have our eye on Russia."

Readers of Swinburne's poetry know that, for a poet, he was exceptionally interested in politics.

They might think, however, that his interest depended on sudden excitements inflaming his patriotism or his republicanism. On the contrary, he was steadily interested in the political affairs of the world and discussed them daily with my husband.

In the progress of science, strangely enough, he took not the faintest interest, and Walter used often to say to me that it was useless to try to discuss a scientific subject with Algernon as it only bored him.

In the afternoon the Bard had the *Pall Mall Gazette*. If that evening paper failed to arrive at its appointed time, he grew quite restless, pacing up and down his room and exhibiting other symptoms of impatience. It came and there was silence. He liked to read the book-notices, and as far as my personal knowledge of his newspaper reading goes, I can vouch for the absorbing interest which he would take in a paragraph, such as would appear now and then in the *Pall Mall Gazette*, recording the death of a centenarian or nonagenarian. When he happened on one, of these stimulating items, he would hurry down to us, paper in hand, and in a joyous mood read and remark on some paragraph like this : " Mrs. So-and-So has just died at the age of ninety-nine in full possession of all her faculties. Ah! How very wonderful! So splendid of her! Quite beats *my aunt Ju.*" Swinburne's "Aunt Ju" was invariably trotted out when remarkably old ladies became a topic of conversation. Miss Julia Swinburne ("Aunt Ju") was one of his favourite aunts and a fine artist. She was a pupil of Turner, and actually painted in the open air when she was nearly ninety. The poet's naïve joy in these simple notices was on one occasion transferred into extravagant anger. He had come across an obituary notice headed " Death of a Centenarian." It was a rather long obituary. So he swooped down upon us before going through it, his face radiant—full of the rapture of a great discovery. He began to read. The providential preservation of the old man's faculties, the facility with which he " read the smallest print without the aid of spectacles"—all these things were added to our stock of useless knowledge. And then came the words—unexpected by us and certainly not anticipated by the reader—" As a youth he had met the Great Napoleon. Ugh!!" Anyone curious to know of what heights of violent vituperation the poetic soul is capable should have heard one of Swinburne's tirades when the name of a Bonaparte was mentioned. Words and combinations of words, weird but picturesque, issued from his mouth like flames from a burning chimney. The old man was forgotten—his centenarianism appealed no more, his " faculties " and his mastery of small print were no longer of the slightest interest. The denunciation to which I listened might have been uttered by a bargee with a liberal knowledge of the beautiful Billingsgate of the Porch. To me the experience had all the delight of novelty, but after several similar exhibitions, I began to wonder how a man could work himself into such a passion about anything as Swinburne invariably achieved at the mention of a Bonaparte. Even Victor Hugo's literary castigation of Napoleon III is mild compared with Swinburne's impromptu diatribes against the first and the last emperors of that name.

The Bard was noticeably addicted to the use of catchwords. Mrs. Gamp supplied him with several. A phrase having struck him as acutely humorous, he would seize upon it, repeat it, domesticate it, so to speak, and thenceforth trot it out on innumerable occasions. One example must suffice here. He was immensely tickled by the remark alleged to have been made by Charlotte Brontë's father when " Jane Eyre " was acclaimed by the critics. The remark, addressed to Emily and Anne, was " Charlotte has been writing a book, and it is much *better than likely.*" This afforded the poet ecstasies of delight. He disliked parsons, and he rejoiced in obtaining from the Brontës' clerical father what he regarded as a matchless specimen of critical and parsonical ineptitude. Hence when some remarkable work was mentioned in the Bard's presence, he immediately fired off his " it is much better than likely " or " it's rather better than likely " with all the pleasure of a schoolboy conscious of doing something impish. In moods like this— never displayed before visitors—he was quite adorable.

Very characteristic of him are the marginalia which he occasionally jotted against passages that excited him to comment while reading. As a rule these scribblings were not intended to be critical in any serviceable way; they were, for the most part, mere tokens of a mood, flippant or not as the case might be. Perhaps the note would be merely an interjection. From this you would infer just how the passage opposite to it had affected him. He hated anything unctuous or hypocritical. When he wished to indicate a passage which struck him as reeking abominably of oily hypocrisy, he would write on the margin, "Ah! " An ironic use of "Alas! " appears elsewhere ; and, opposite a text of Scripture quoted in a pamphlet, he has written *à la* Mrs. Gamp, " Sich was his Bible language ! "

How many things come back to me now as I gaze into the deserted garden !

CHAPTER XI

THE BARD AS A MAN OF BUSINESS

IN some respects Algernon Swinburne was quite business-like. In the ordering of his daily life he was as methodical as a city man. His hours were fixed and he was punctuality itself in observing them. He knew the place of every book on every shelf in his library. His manuscript was always ready to his hand. If he laid down a book he had been reading, he would take it up again, perhaps days afterwards, and re-commence reading at the place where he had left off. Were method and punctuality the only qualities demanded from a man of affairs, his equipment would have been perfect. But there are others essential to the complete city man. And in these he was deficient.

Money holds a very important place in the transactions of business men—even where money does not pass in coin or cheques. I have been told that a mere nod from a great financial operator may mean the transfer of hundreds of thousands of pounds. To the poet such a tale would appeal only as an example of Oriental magic, if indeed he did not dismiss it as grotesque. In the small monetary transactions of daily life the Bard was hopelessly incompetent. To him money was merely good hard coin. I believe the paper currency of to-day would have maddened him, and that John Bradbury or N. K. Warren Fisher would have become the constant object of his picturesque vituperation. Amounts on paper were unrealities to him. His neglect of dividend warrants and publishers' cheques was amazing.

Here for instance is a letter—there are others of a similar kind—from his long-suffering publishers. It is dated 10th January, 1901·

Dear Mr. Swinburne,

On looking through our pass-book, we noted that the cheque we sent you for £200-11-9, drawn in your favour on July 5th, 1900, for royalties then due, has not been passed into the bankers, although the one for £115-9-9 which we sent you last week, has been duly presented and paid.

As our previous cheque may have been lost, or inadvertently overlooked, we think it best to bring the matter under your notice. We shall be happy to issue a duplicate if you are unable to lay your hands upon the missing cheque—which we shall then instruct our bankers to cancel, should it by any chance hereafter be presented to them for payment.

> With kind regards,
>
> We are, dear Mr. Swinburne,
>
> Yours very faithfully,
>
> CHATTO & WINDUS.

I am not in a position to say what reply was sent to this particular letter, but it is certain that even a letter of this kind, a model of courtesy, would sometimes excite Swinburne to wrath. It would interrupt and bore him; and, hating to be interrupted, or bored, he would consign, in a burst of rhetoric, publishers and bankers, their methods and their persons to every conceivable sort of Inferno. But this explosion would not be followed by any attempt to make a search for the missing document. Nor was the polite letter from the publishers usually regarded by him as anything calling for reply or acknowledgment. Eventually, and in despair, the firm would write to my husband imploring his assistance and advice. A search would then be made, and the cheque would, perhaps, be discovered tucked away with any old rubbish; or perhaps the document would have disappeared from the face of the earth and the promised duplicate would be forwarded in due course.

Swinburne's relations with Messrs. Chatto and Windus were fundamentally excellent. They were his publishers from 1878 to his death, and Mr. Andrew Chatto attended his funeral.

I have said enough concerning the poet's ineptitude as a man of business. I have now to speak of the business faculty which he showed in arranging his life's routine at The Pines. The programme was his own, laid down in the days when he and my husband were both bachelors, and it was adhered to with pathetic fidelity. Nor was there anything in the assignment of hours that called for alteration when I—little more than a girl in years—became *châtelaine* at The Pines.

At about ten o'clock a.m. the poet came down from his bedroom and went into his library on the first floor. Here breakfast was at once served. He desired always to breakfast alone. One of his little fads was to have his coffee made in an old silver coffee-pot, engraved with his initials, his companion since his not particularly joyous 'Varsity days. He then glanced at the daily paper. At eleven o'clock or thereabouts he was ready for his walk to Wimbledon. This, I think, was to him the great event of the day. He thoroughly enjoyed the exercise, and to his business-like regularity in adhering to this daily practice must be mainly attributed the excellent health he enjoyed. He went out in all weathers. He absolutely refused to encumber himself with an overcoat, umbrella or gloves. One might as well have offered an umbrella to an antelope or mountain goat.

Towards one-thirty, he returned from his walk, rushed upstairs to his bedroom with the elasticity and noise of a boy, and changed all his under-garments. The poet's laundry bill was a formidable document—such dozens of shirts! Swinburne's passionate desire for personal cleanliness is inconsistent with artistic Bohemia and its traditions. Fresh as the proverbial daisy, at half-past one he would bound into the dining-room, ready for lunch, and eager to talk of his adventures, his purchases, and his experiences generally.

Here, as illustrating a self-control with which he is seldom credited, I record his avoidance of those dishes which he knew from experience were not good for him. For instance, he avoided shell-fish, although he liked it. Lobster or crab was never served. I remember once buying some aspic jelly which I made into moulds with very pink shrimps showing through the gelatinous transparency. He was immensely pleased with the appearance of the dainty. " How very pretty those little things look—almost too pretty to eat!" was his comment. " 'But I think I *must* this time because *you* prepared it."

Lunch at an end, the next item was the siesta. For this he retired to his bedroom. It lasted until about four, at which hour he descended to his library and read or wrote until six. Next to that of his morning walk, six o'clock was the hour he anticipated with the greatest delight. Punctually to the minute, he would announce himself in our sitting-room downstairs, armed with the volume in which he was interested at the time. It was usually a work of Dickens—for the poet was a devoted Dickensian. At first, let me confess, the evening reading bored me, and I frequently avoided being present. But when I saw the pleasure that reciting his favourite " bits " afforded the poet, I submitted with a good grace and even experienced a sort of reflected pleasure in the exercise, although the function usually lasted for an hour and three-quarters—something of a trial for one who is young and accustomed to the ordinary pleasures of youth.

THE HOME LIFE OF SWINBURNE

At eight o'clock, the reading having lasted until a quarter to that hour, we moved to the dining-room for the evening meal, and, that being over, Swinburne went up to his library to browse among his books.

Such was the daily routine, and my husband was anxious that it should be observed with the most religious particularity. Any slight departure from the daily round affected Walter more than it affected his friend. My husband never exhibited any signs of annoyance or impatience, but I, who read him, *knew*. For himself it mattered nothing. All his fear was lest the Bard should be " put out " by any slight departure from the appointed happenings. The visits of friends, either of Swinburne or of my husband, were not permitted to make any difference in the settled programme. " The Hours " were regarded as sacred at The Pines.

Although the Bard exhibited a really unheard-of carelessness in dealing with cheques for consider-able sums, he had a curious business instinct in asserting his commercial rights in small matters. For instance, when he ordered a recently-published book he always demanded the once obtainable discount of three pence in the shilling. And when he ordered an old book from a catalogue, he declined to refund the postage, observing that the bookseller from whom he ordered received from the dealer a commission which should cover any charges of carriage. Not so bad for a poet, I have often thought.

I end this chapter with an amusing example of his more peculiar methods of transacting business. He loathed coppers in change—unless they were quite new and bright. This dislike was not, I imagine, mere caprice, but arose from that passion for cleanliness which was part of his nature. Coppers looked dirty, and probably were associated in his mind with the dirty hands and dirty pockets with which they had come into contact during circulation. Now, he purchased at Wimbledon every day a copy of the *Daily Graphic*. It was not always convenient to buy five penny-worth of something else and so make up the sum to six-pence. So between them the accommodating newsagent and the poet hit upon the following device. On Monday morning Swinburne would tender a sixpence for his daily newspaper, and the vendor would give him in change five beautiful new pennies. These he placed in a waistcoat pocket by themselves and on each of the five succeeding days of the week he would tender a penny out of this reserve, which would of course be exhausted on the Saturday. Then on the following Monday a sixpence would again be tendered, and a similar set of clean pennies be given in change.

Swinburne's explanation to the newsvendor of this method of purchase was softened by the remark that the five pennies made a sort of coin-calendar for the week. When the waistcoat pocket was empty, he knew that the day was Saturday and that the dreaded Sunday loomed ahead.

A business man—of sorts—was the poet, but a boy always.

CHAPTER XII

SWINBURNE'S HUMOUR

SAVE in the brilliant parodies collected in " The Heptalogia," there is little trace of humour in the poetry of Swinburne. Even in the dramas it is very sparingly employed. His prose contains witty passages and even a disguised " Limerick," yet the general impression left by the perusal of Swinburne's works is not that of a naturally humorous person. The fact is, however, that he possessed a keen sense of humour. Like his other gifts, his humour was Swinburnian, in other words, his own. As I recall it now, it appears to have had three principal manifestations. There was his mordant humour ; his playful humour ; his practical humour.

I shall pass lightly over the first of these. It was reserved for persons or things distasteful to him. He was that " good hater " for whom Dr.

Johnson professed a love. Indeed, I very much question whether the great lexicographer ever met a man quite as eloquent as Swinburne in the expression of his hatred. I sometimes felt as I heard him that he did not really hate the victim so much as his language implied. When he heartily meant his abuse, there was no mistaking the animus behind his words. Picturesque, extravagant, and full of unexpected phrases, his denunciations were delightful to those whose withers were not wrung. Often they would send Walter and me into fits of laughter, laughter in which the Bard would join with the utmost abandon. These exhibitions of humorous wrath were much less charming when they were made in conversation with visitors. They had whatever fun could be got out of his unsparing severity to offending contemporaries, but they were not regaled by any playfulness : they heard or saw none of those inimitable imitations of the idiosyncrasies of his victim which we of the household were privileged to enjoy. Before the stranger within the gates he set bounds to his fancies. With us he " let himself go."

I refrain from mentioning the names of persons still living at whom he was accustomed to fling his humorous gibes. But of those who have died

SWINBURNE'S HUMOUR

I may mention Mr. James Anthony Froude as the subject of some of his most amusing outbursts. Swinburne simply loathed Froude, and if ridicule could kill, the eminent historian would have been gathered to his fathers long before the date at which he joined the great majority. I suppose—though the poet never actually said so—that his hatred of Froude was aroused originally by that historian's description of the person and estimate of the character of Mary, Queen of Scots.

Swinburne's playful humour was called forth by incidents he witnessed during his morning rambles and also by items in the daily papers. He would hunt about in odd corners for those little " fill-up " paragraphs which the general reader is apt to overlook. His " finds " in this field were an unfailing source of interest and mirth. He would rush down to us when he found something that tickled his fancy, read out the precious paragraph, fire off a humorous comment, and rush off again.

Nothing amused him more than the proceeding of the Church Congress when that ecclesiastical assembly held its meetings at the Albert Hall; or perhaps I should say that nothing amused him so much as the letters appearing in the correspondence columns of the *Daily Telegraph* commenting on those proceedings. These letters were a real joy to him day after day, and when they ceased, he was quite gloomy for a time. The letters from curates on such subjects as " The Cure of Souls " and " Disheartened Clergy " he read and re-read. He caught the ordinary Oxford-bred curate's brassy tone with wonderful accuracy. I can recall even now his rendering of a passage from a correspondent who was not a clergyman. Swinburne gave it out with a wicked joyousness. The writer said :—" There are rectors who in a very few years have contrived to make almost every member of their flock hate the inside of a Church."

When I complimented A. C. S. on his really fine imitation of a priest intoning, " Did you not know," he asked, " that I disappointed my family by not entering the Church? Can you not imagine Walter and myself in Holy Orders?"—this with a perfectly idiotic sigh. It struck me at the moment as being merely a joke. Walter subsequently informed me, however, that it was a statement of sober truth. The Church, I am sure, did not lose much ; and the world has gained, *inter alia*, the " Hymn to Proserpine," which would scarcely have been in good taste had it come from the study of a curate, in spite of the fact that we are indebted to a Catholic priest for the beautiful story of " Manon Lescaut."

SWINBURNE'S HUMOUR

By Swinburne's practical humour I do not mean elaborated practical joking of the kind that Theodore Hook and E. A. Sothern indulged in. Swinburne's practical jokes usually took a literary turn. I select a couple of examples, in both of which his object was apparently to excite my surprise and curiosity concerning something which in itself was not likely to arouse emotion of any sort.

The first of these jokes occurred some time after my marriage, when the poet and I were on perfectly easy terms. He came downstairs one evening holding a little book. He seldom arrived without a book, big or little, in his hand. He proposed to read to us from " The Seven Poor Travellers " of Dickens. Swinburne's face was much more easy to read than some of the books on his shelves. And it was not difficult to see now that there was mischief of some sort brewing. There was an air of mystery about him as he glanced with a sly expression from Walter to me. In this instance it was not with me a case of " forewarned, forearmed." The joke came off, and I was fairly " had "—as Cockneys say.

He opened the little book and made what lecturers call " a few preliminary remarks " on the peculiar merits of " The Seven Poor Travellers " and the brutal density of readers of

Dickens who know nothing of this wonderful little work of his. The ignorance of the average reader did not appear to me so extraordinary when he told us that the work consisted of eight chapters—the first and the last being by Charles Dickens and the other six by members of the staff of *Household Words*, of which "The Seven Poor Travellers" was issued as á Christmas number. George Augustus Sala and Wilkie Collins were among the contributors. Both these writers were favourites with the poet. For Sala's work he always professed a tremendous admiration—a circumstance which will come as a blow to those devotees who picture the Bard as eternally wallowing either in Hugo or in Elizabethan and Jacobean drama. And a sight of the rows of "yellow backs" in Swinburne's bedroom would probably have horrified those who imagined that only "the old nobility" of the world of books was interesting to him.

To return, however, to my anecdote: having concluded his prefatory remarks, Swinburne began to read. The opening sentence to "The Seven Poor Travellers" goes thus:

Strictly speaking there were only six Poor Travellers; but being a traveller myself, though an idle one, and being withal as poor as I hope to be, I brought the number up

to seven. This word of explanation is due at once, for
what says the inscription over the quaint old door?

RICHARD WATTS, ESQ.,
by his Will dated 22 Aug. 1597
founded this charity
for Six Poor Travellers,
who not being ROGUES or PROCTORS,
May secure gratis for one NIGHT
Lodging, Entertainment,
and Four pence each.

All this elaborate prefacing, this air of mystifica-
tion seemed to enhance the effect of a substitution
of one Christian name for another in the first line
of the inscription relating to the charity of the
eccentric Rochester testator. Swinburne paused
before he perpetrated his joke. A flush appeared
on his cheeks. His eyes twinkled. Then he
uttered the words " *Walter* Watts " I confess
I was completely taken in. I was in no sense of
the word a Dickensian ; and before Swinburne
read it, was utterly ignorant of " The Seven Poor
Travellers."

Taking his manner in connection with the matter
which he had read to us, I came to the conclusion
that the Walter Watts of the altered inscription
was some ancestor of the Walter Theodore Watts
to whom I was married—the very misconception

which Swinburne meant to create. His joke
having succeeded, he took no further liberties
with Dickens's text. It was not until Swinburne
left the room that I discovered how he had
imposed upon me.

The Bard's second attempt to get off a little joke
at my expense was not so successful as its fore-
runner. One day Walter asked me to read out
to him from " Chambers's Cyclopædia of English
Literature " the account given of Maturin, the
author of " Melmoth the Wanderer." I had just
finished doing this when Swinburne came into the
room. He looked over my shoulder to see what
I had been reading. His eye caught, on the top
of the page preceding that upon which I had been
at work, the name Matthew Gregory Lewis.
Instead of plunging into the merits and demerits
of " Melmoth," as I had half expected he would
have done, he politely asked me to give him the
volume. As he took it, he said, " I should so
much like to read you *the* most wonderful ballad
of the Eighteenth Century." I professed myself
delighted and was preparing myself for the enjoy-
ment of an intellectual treat. However, I noticed
that the two friends exchanged glances. My
husband had his tongue in his cheek, and
Swinburne's eyes were beginning to dance with

mischief. I recognised the symptoms. Experience had made me wary. I was not to be " had " a second time.

As was his wont he began with a little prelude. He explained the properties of the ballad, and desired that in listening to this example of ballad literature I should pay particular attention to the awful fate that overtook the heroine. I dare say a good many readers know the poem. Some of them, perhaps, like it. But few, I imagine, ever got a tenth part of the fun out of it that Swinburne did on that occasion. His only failure was in pretending that he was dealing with " the most wonderful ballad of the Eighteenth Century." For I knew " Alonzo the Brave and the Fair Imogene " perfectly well, and, with all my limitations, was capable of noting the difference between the dross and the gold of literature. Swinburne exhibited unbounded humour in his delivery of this grotesquely sensational poem. As its vogue is over, I quote two of its seventeen stanzas. The ballad begins ·

A warrior so bold, and a virgin so bright,
   Conversed as they sat on the green;
They gazed on each other with tender delight:
Alonzo the Brave was the name of the Knight—
   The maiden's the Fair Imogene.

And this is the last stanza :

> While they drink out of skulls newly torn from the grave,
>   Dancing round them the spectres are seen;
> Their liquor is blood, and this horrible stave
> They howl: " To the health of Alonzo the Brave,
>   And his consort, the Fair Imogene."

" Monk " Lewis here brought gruesomeness to a climax. His ballad naturally lends itself to burlesque, and in burlesque I first made its acquaintance. But no burlesque of this " most wonderful ballad " could outdo Swinburne's serio-comic rendering. He seemed to revel in the grim idiocy of Lewis's incidents and situations. He had enough sympathy with the *macabre* to take some gruesome stories seriously; but Alonzo and Imogene were altogether too much for his sense of the ludicrous to remain dormant under the provocation of their remarkable woes. The tone he adopted in rendering the lines which he most desired to ridicule resembled the peculiar unctuous drawl of an intoning curate—the long O's being dwelt on and drawn out in a highly diverting manner.

He achieved a *tour de force* in the recitation of the crowning stanza, which he made a crescendo of gruesome horror. I shall never forget that amazing performance. The Bard as an entertainer was at his best. The accidental nature of the reading increased its charm. I never heard him revert to Lewis's ballad again; but this single recitation was enough to prove to me beyond all doubt that Swinburne's sense of humour was exceptionally keen and alert.

CHAPTER XIII

SWINBURNE THE DICKENSIAN

ANY description of the home life of Swinburne that omitted to mention Dickens, would be grievously incomplete. The author of the " Pickwick Papers " was simply adored by the poet, who was as much at extremes in his admirations as in his dislikes. My husband also admired the great Victorian novelist's works, though in a less ardent degree. Thus, during my married life, I lived more or less in a Dickens atmosphere, but I was born more than a decade too late to share the enthusiasm of those who read Dickens while he was still alive. I had escaped the glamour which " the inimitable " shed upon contemporaries. I belong to a generation which has set up other demigods, the worship of whom would be regarded by the true Dickensian as mere idolatry.

Nevertheless, I can understand the devotional

enthusiasm of those who lived while Dickens was still writing, putting forth—as he himself expressed it—his two green leaves a month. They would feel, as younger people could not, the truth to life of Dickens's characters, and the realism of the descriptions of scenes which have changed. The great " Dust Heap " of oblivion which, like Mr. Boffin's mounds, are supposed to contain so much that is valuable, is not a dust heap to everybody. The contemporaries of Dickens breathed his atmosphere. We others are mentally too removed from it to enjoy it as perhaps it deserves.

Unfortunately the Dickens readings to which Swinburne so insistently treated us were not at all calculated to create an enthusiasm. Even his recitation of the dialogues between Sarah Gamp and Betsy Prig failed to move me and the amours of Mrs. Corney and the Beadle left me cold. At school I had gone through a course of elocution. I had " taken " to it, and was reported by my instructor to show unusual aptitude. Therefore, my attitude to reciters was, in a way, that of an expert. When I found that, in his rendering of Dickens, A. C. S. ruthlessly disregarded all the rules of the game as I had been taught to play it, I was first surprised, then bored, but finally—such is the influence of a remarkable person, apart from the success or failure of what he happens to be doing when one observes him—I became interested.

Swinburne's voice was curiously unsuited to the interpretation of Dickens. I was amazed to read that he possessed a " rich contralto! " To my thinking the quality of his voice was distinctly male, verging on falsetto when he was excited and on its high notes. At its best, it was musical and sometimes tender. He did not command many tones, and his voice, in later life at any rate, had an ineradicable metallic quality which interfered with its flexibility. And when the reader was carried away by the pathos or the passion or the rollicking humour of his author, he had a tendency to rise to a kind of involuntary shriek unpleasant to hear.

I confess that I went through a stage of boredom during these readings from Dickens—one might almost say, these Dickensian devotions. Happily this stage did not last long. The unalloyed satisfaction, sometimes intensified to obvious rapture, which the reading of his favourite writer of fiction gave the poet, evoked a sympathetic response from his audience of two One could not witness his

excessive affection for the Dickens characters
without being moved by a kindred feeling.   In
spite of his natural defects as an elocutionist,
Swinburne's peculiar manner of reading grew
upon you. You endured, you tolerated, and at
last you enjoyed and looked forward to it.

Moreover, his elocutionary exhibitions gave me
furiously to think. How came it that a man of
Swinburne's temperament, tastes, classical equipment, and high poetic achievement should have
come so completely under the thraldom of
Dickens? What in the name of wonder could the
author of "Atalanta in Calydon" and "Ave
atque Vale" have in common with the writer of
"Martin Chuzzlewit" and the "Pickwick
Papers"?

Some minor resemblances I have not failed to
note. Both these great writers, for instance,
wrote from time to time in dramatic form.
Neither wrote successfully for the stage. Here
let me point out that it has been stated that
"Locrine" was the only work by Swinburne to
be played in his lifetime, whereas the fact is that
"Atalanta" was staged in 1907, although he
himself took precious little interest in the
production. It is quite true that in his later years
A. C. S. disclaimed any desire to see his plays

staged. 'Almost the only time that I knew him to be cross with me was in connection with his uncomplimentary attitude to the theatre. He had been reading to me from " The Duke of Gandia," and when he came to the culminating point of the wonderful last act, I could not help exclaiming, " What a splendid curtain! " He put down the book, regarded me freezingly, and said in a tone of grave rebuke, " I never write for the stage " I knew him pretty well by this time. I knew all about the attempt that had been made to get " Bothwell " acted—had indeed pored over a copy of that work which had been cut about, altered, and enriched by stage directions. So I did not take the rebuke lying down. On the contrary, I stood up to the poet, argued the point with him, and saw his little mood of irritation pass and his old boyish spirit return. He was quite abashed at having had the temerity to rebuke me, and when I told him that both Walter and I considered " Chastelard " had splendid dramatic moments and ought to be put on the boards, he looked extremely pleased and never attempted to contradict me.

Both Dickens and Swinburne loved an audience. Swinburne would go on reading to an audience of two persons for hours. Dickens, as is well known, made large sums of money by his public readings. The difference between the readers was of course greatly in favour of the novelist. Dickens was a born actor. His voice, we have been told, was capable of wonderful inflections and his mastery over the sympathies of his audience magnetic and irresistible. Almost all that Dickens *was* in this respect Swinburne was *not.* But the attitude towards the audience in both men was the same.

What are known as " socialistic leanings " characterised both the novelist and the poet. Both had ideals and envisaged a socialism that would ameliorate the condition of the poor without putting an undue strain on the social system as it exists. And I imagine that the socialism both of Dickens and Swinburne was founded quite as much on hatred of the rich as on affection for the needy. They both harboured unkindly feelings towards the wealthy. Dickens has revealed his attitude in Podsnap, Parsons, Mr and Mrs. Merdle and Bounderby. He had no use whatever for plutocrats, unless, like the Cheeryble Brothers in " Nicholas Nickleby," they distributed their gains to the deserving poor. But Swinburne's detestation of the rich was founded on no excessive love for their less fortunate brothers. In principle he made common cause with the proletariat. In practice the needs of the people troubled him no more than the claims of the equator. His abstract hatred of rich men was, however, very real. He would, if the man possessed compensating qualities, just tolerate the inheritor of riches. But for the citizen who had made money in trade or in the city he harboured the feeling of deadly malevolence. Some of the most eloquent denunciatory outbursts I have heard from him were on this subject. He did not value money himself. He detested all those who did.

Perhaps the reader will be inclined to smile when I say that another point of resemblance between Swinburne and Dickens is that both the great writers were poets. True, Dickens was a poet only in a small way, and I do not rest his poetic claim on his occasional lyrics—" The Ivy Green " for example—but on his prose. Here he sang unconsciously. One has only to read the account of the funeral of Little Nell in "The Old Curiosity Shop" to be assured of this. It is rhythmical throughout, and with very slight alteration could be arranged to run its course in blank verse. This was pointed out to me by my husband. I have, I confess, never heard Swinburne's views on the subject. But it is reasonable to infer that the rhythmical quality

SWINBURNE AT THE AGE OF FOUR

of much of Dickens's prose appealed to the Bard and cemented the sympathy which he extended to everything Dickens wrote.

In English fiction Dickens was his first love. In that small space of his life covered by his expression " When I was a kid at Eton," the time during which the Master was still putting out his " two green leaves " a month, he came under the Dickens spell, and he remained under it to the last. He had the same sort of affection—if less in degree—for Dickens that he entertained for those members of his family who were the companions of his boyhood. He admired Scott. He venerated Hugo. He loved Dickens.

I agree with those critics who regard Swinburne's book, " Charles Dickens," as an unsatisfactory performance. It could scarcely be anything else, made up, as it is, of two " commissioned " articles. It does not adequately inform us of the writer's preferences. It is not a scientific piece of criticism. It is literary adulation—eloquent, interesting, but hardly illuminative. One or two examples of critical insight redeem the essay. He thinks, for instance, that Little Nell in " The Old Curiosity Shop " and Oliver Twist in the novel of the same name are too good to be true to nature. Oliver, indeed, he dismisses as " rather too like the literary son and heir of a maiden lady."

Sarah Gamp was one of his prime favourites. He revelled in her conversational eccentricities. It mattered not how often her aphorisms were quoted by him, they never failed to excite him to ecstasies of mirth. One passage was a particular favourite of his. I can hear him now repeating it, and I can catch an echo of the unrestrained laughter that followed its delivery. I confess it always failed to tickle my own sense of humour. This is the passage : " ' I have know'd that sweetest and best of women,' said Mrs. Gamp, shaking her head and shedding tears, ' ever since afore her First, which Mr. Harris who was dreadful timid went and stopped his ears in a empty dog-kennel, and never took his hands away or come out once till he was showed the baby, wen bein' took with fits, the doctor collared him and laid him on his back upon the airy stones, and she was told to ease her mind, his owls was organs.' " I accustomed myself to join in the laughter that followed the recitation, feeling all the while that I was an awful hypocrite. For a time the cryptic statement " his owls was organs " interested me. But Walter translated the sentence into English for me, and after that, even the owls and organs failed to stir me to the slightest enthusiasm.

Wilkins Micawber and Dick Swiveller were persons whose views and adventures possessed an unfailing attraction for the poet. He seemed to regard them rather as friends with whom he had been associated all his life than as mere *dramatis personæ* in works of fiction. When he referred to them, it was as though he were speaking of living contemporaries. But of all the characters in the whole range of the Dickens creation none appealed so surely and directly to Swinburne's sense of humour as one who never appears in person on the novelist's stage—who is heard of but never seen. I refer to Old Bill Barley in "Great Expectations." Bill Barley, it will be remembered, is a bed-ridden old blasphemer "with the gout in his right hand—and everywhere else."

Old Barley's sustained growl vibrated in the beam that crossed the ceiling." "The growl swelled into a roar again and a frightful bumping noise was heard above, as if a giant with a wooden leg was trying to bore it through the ceiling to come at us."

The particular passage that Swinburne loved to repeat—and how often I have heard him!—was this: "As we passed Mr. Barley's door, he was heard hoarsely muttering within, in a strain that rose and fell like the wind, the following refrain, in which I substitute good wishes for something quite the reverse: 'Ahoy! Bless your eyes, here's old Bill Barley. Here's old Bill Barley, bless your eyes. Here's old Bill Barley on the flat of his back, by the Lord. Lying on the flat of his back, like a drifting old dead flounder, here's your old Bill Barley, bless your eyes. Ahoy! Bless you!' " Swinburne used to give this with immense unction and emphasis, supplying in place of the innocuous " Bless you " the form of objurgation which old Bill Barley may have been supposed to employ. In Bill Barley, Swinburne had probably encountered a kindred spirit, for as I have already said, his own vituperative vocabulary was most picturesque and was practically unlimited. But with the magnanimity of true genius he permitted Bill Barley to " go one better." Whenever he had finished his rendering of Barley's comminatory growl, he invariably indulged in warmly appreciative comments, such as, " What a wealth of language! " " How wonderful! " " What a magnificent gift of metaphor! " It was impossible to say how much of this commendation was intended to be taken seriously. But his affection for the gouty old reprobate was unaffected and sincere, and the Bill Barley monologue was one of Swinburne's most cherished " bits."

If Bill Barley was the character most endeared to A. C. S., the novel in which Barley appears— or rather in which he does *not* appear—was his favourite book of the Dickens series. He greatly loved " David Copperfield," but on the whole he perhaps admired most " Great Expectations." And there is a great deal to be said in favour of Swinburne's choice. The monstrously unnatural figure and absurdly unconvincing surroundings of Miss Havisham, overshadow the pages and give an air of unreality to the whole narrative. But take out Miss Havisham altogether and enough remains to justify and account for Swinburne's preference. Jaggers and Wemmick, Joe Gargery, and Mr. Pumblechook, Orlick and Magwitch— these are creations worthy of a great novelist. And the story itself shows evidences of constructive power which seem to me to be singularly absent in those earlier works of Dickens which are considered his best. The narrative proceeds without prolixity and has artistic merits which are relatively rare. On the whole then, Swinburne's selection of " Great Expectations " is justifiable.

CHAPTER XIV

CHRISTMAS AT THE PINES

In this chapter I will endeavour to describe my first Christmas (that of 1905) at The Pines in the company of Algernon Swinburne, and as it resembles other equally joyous Christmases spent under the same roof, this one may be regarded as typical of all.

Alas! my inability to use more than a tyro's skill in painting my picture demands that the reader shall use his own imagination to assist him to visualise a scene worthy of the pen of Dickens himself. Indeed my recollection of Christmas at The Pines mainly concerns the influence that " the Master " exercised in our household at and about December 25th.

We had a perfect glut of Dickens then. To me it was a revelation : the idolatry by two poets of a personage whom I only knew through the medium of two or three novels. To Swinburne and Walter, Dickens stood for the very spirit of Christmas itself, and everything they did, and a great deal they said, echoed the feelings with which he animated them.

Sometimes I ask myself which of the two friends did the most in bringing the Dickens atmosphere into the home. One thing is clear: Swinburne was mad—I can use no other term— about nearly everything that Dickens wrote. When he was regaling us with " Martin Chuzzlewit " it was apparent that he knew long passages of it by heart, so little did he seem to rely on the book open before him.

Walter, with less exuberance, shared Swinburne's admiration, and it was chiefly owing to his desire to gratify his housemate and at the same time to honour the famous dead, that the Christmas anniversary at The Pines became a Dickens festival. Though Swinburne enjoyed it all, he was certainly not the magician who permeated our home with the Christmassy atmosphere of revelry. I cannot picture *him* paying homage to Dickens by planning a Christmas programme according to the traditions of Boz. It was Walter who kept the torch of good fellowship burning, and who—so it seemed to me—was symbolical of the genial Mr. Wardle of " Pickwick."

THE HOME LIFE OF SWINBURNE

It was for me very new and wonderful, this idea of celebrating Christmas in the good old-fashioned manner, hitherto only known to me by what I had read in books or seen illustrated in the Christmas annuals. And this idea of bringing in Dickens— a genial ghost—as the presiding genius, seemed to me delightfully unique.

Strangely enough, the zest of the two friends in Christmas was just as keen as when they first celebrated it at The Pines in precisely the same way twenty-six years before. Here, in 1879, as they stood together before the Christmas tree of little five-year old Bertie Mason,* they both vowed that whatever of good or ill-fortune the passing year had brought to them, Christmas would always find them young in heart and spirit.

Walter wrote a sonnet to celebrate the occasion, and as it describes far more clearly than I can in what attitude of mind both Swinburne and he regarded the closing of the passing year, I quote it here :

Life still hath one romance that naught can bury—
　　Not Time himself, who coffins Life's romances—
　　For still will Christmas gild the year's mischances,
If Childhood comes, as here, to make him merry—

* The hero of Swinburne's " Dark Month."

CHRISTMAS AT THE PINES

To kiss with lips more ruddy than the cherry—
    To smile with eyes outshining by their glances
    The Christmas tree—to dance with fairy dances
And crown his hoary head with leaf and berry.

And as for us, dear friend, the carols sung
    Are fresh as ever. Bright is yonder bough
Of mistletoe as that which shone and swung
    When you and I and Friendship made a vow
    That Childhood's Christmas still should seal each brow—
Friendship's, and yours, and mine—and keep us young.

This vow the poets had literally and spiritually kept, and the festival was looked forward to by them with a joy resembling that of a schoolboy home for the holidays. The delights of anticipation were apparent in their childlike demeanour; the years were rolled behind them, and many traits of the boy peeped out in them at this season. *They* were never too old for Santa Claus.

As the season advanced Swinburne would notice during his walks if the holly trees promised a good supply of red berries. If they did, he would remark with all the glee of a ten-year old youngster, " I expect there'll be a lovely lot of berries on the holly this Christmas."

One fact that made this particular Christmas stand out for me in bold and happy relief was that it was the Christmas directly after my marriage,

which had only taken place in the preceding month.
Oh! the delights of shopping with Walter in the
late December afternoons. My mind, reverting
to them, brings back a score of golden memories.
It was at dusk when the shops are brilliantly lighted
that he preferred to saunter with me in busy and
crowded Oxford Street and Regent Street. Many
a precious hour did we waste gazing into shop
windows at the temptations offered to our purse;
but we voted the time well spent, and Walter considered it part of my education as a budding
Dickensian to observe and take full advantage of
the interesting scenes going on around us.

As we marched gaily along, he regaled me with
anecdotes of Old Scrooge and Bob Cratchit, so
that I could mentally see these Christmas creations
of the Master's fancy. Walter amused himself
by imagining whence the people came whom we
saw staring at the shops. These, he would say,
were from the country; those from the East End;
in each case the West End was their paradise of
sightseeing. When we came across a shabby man
accompanied by a swarm of children whose noses
were glued to a shop window, he would nudge my
arm and remark, " Look, there goes the worthy
Bob and the little Cratchits."

There was fun, too, in returning home in the

evening with our purchases, and finding Swinburne placidly ensconced in his cosy sitting-room, quite unaware that all the afternoon we had formed a part of London's jostling crowd of shoppers. To imagine him one of them was impossible. Nevertheless, he did do Christmas shopping, though not with crowds. He did it in his own leisurely way. For years he pursued the same course, going about it calmly and methodically in easy stages during his walks to Wimbledon.

As Christmas approached he selected with great care the gifts and cards he intended for his friends and relations. There was something rather charming about this proceeding on the part of one who so heartily detested writing letters or transacting business of any sort. He even found a keen pleasure in his Christmas shopping, and gave himself a lot of trouble about it. He never thought of adopting the modern habit of ordering so many dozens of the same card with the sender's name and address printed thereon. On the contrary, he made a distinct choice in the purchase of each individual card.

In his arduous task he invariably called upon Miss Frost of the Wimbledon book-shop to assist him. He would sally forth across the Common, the end he had in view imparting a spice of mystery and adventure to his walk. We were not supposed to know what was going on, and it was not until the day before Christmas that anybody knew the nature of his purchases. Then he would gleefully show what he had been at such pains to procure. He would show me first the Christmas card he had got for Walter, asking me meanwhile not to tell him. In a like manner he would tell Walter not to say a word that he had also got one for me " hidden up his sleeve."

He always seemed quite pleased with everything he had bought, yet he appeared uncertain as to what the recipient would think of the little gifts. He would enquire anxiously, " Do you think he " (or " she " as the case might be) " will like it? " On being reassured on this head, he would give a little satisfied sigh, as if the question were quite momentous, and murmur with relief, " Oh, I'm so glad you think so too ! "

I remember once how excited he was about a card he had bought for Walter. No child could have looked more pleased at finding the toy he had sighed for in his " Christmas stocking." It was a tiny reproduction of Turner's " Fighting Téméraire tugged to her last berth to be broken up." Swinburne's joy at having secured it was something to remember. He was as pleased as Punch. His amazement at seeing one of his favourite pictures beautifully printed on a fourpenny card was unbounded, and his exclamations of surprise were astonishing. He wanted to know how it could possibly be done for the money, and deemed himself fortunate in obtaining such a bargain. " I wonder what Walter will say about it? " he exclaimed. " I think it is a perfect little masterpiece. I do hope he will like it," etc., etc. These ecstatic phrases were repeated as he gazed at his prize. Even in the matter of choosing Christmas cards as in the case of babies and "the insuperable sea," he showed a curious tendency to believe that everybody's tastes must coincide with his own. Because *he* adored the sea, he imagined all the Universe must do likewise, and he rarely bought a card that did not bear witness to the fact; he once declared in a letter to Clarence Stedman, when speaking of this passion, " Its salt *must* have been in my blood before I was born."

At Christmas time the little shop at Wimbledon was crowded with customers, so the poet would make straight for the owner's private parlour adjoining. Here, secure from interruption and offensive observation, he would sit at a table apart, and leisurely turn over the cards on a tray set before him. "Show me anything with ships on it," he would say; and if by some lucky chance a ship in full sail ploughing the main revealed itself, it was seized upon with avidity and borne off in triumph. But he was not always successful in procuring just what he wanted; and when the card-trays failed to yield the harvest he desired, he would abruptly leave his seat and stalk out of the parlour, murmuring to Miss Fost as he passed through the shop, "I don't see anything else I like." Next day he would return and enthusiastically resume the search, hopeful, as his friend Micawber of immortal memory, of "something turning up."

But Swinburne's quest for cards was a small affair compared with the far more enthralling and important task of selecting Christmas presents. These nearly always took the form of books, which, by the way, he was apt to bestow on his favourites at any time in the year. But at Christmas he let himself go with a lavish hand and always chose expensive books. If an attractive book was displayed on Miss Frost's counter, it did not require much conjecture on the part of the book-seller as to who would be likely to buy it. Directly the poet entered he was automatically attracted towards it. He would take it up, and after looking through it attentively for a while he would say, " This is very nice. I'll take it " But when it came to choosing anything for Walter he was seriously perplexed. He had given that man of innumerable books almost every work he cared to add to such a collection, and it was really difficult to think of something for him which would not be like coals sent to Newcastle. For weeks before Christmas, Swinburne would try to ascertain by all manner of ingenious little devices what book or books would be welcome to Walter. He would pore over catalogues in the hope of finding some treasure he thought might take his friend's fancy.

I can see him now, catalogue in hand, with his finger on the page containing the descriptions of the book he had in mind, his face lit up with the hope that his question, " What do you think of that? " would produce a response favourable to his meditative generosity. But one Christmas a surprise awaited Walter. His present was *not* a book this time !

On one of his pilgrimages Swinburne had espied a bust of his beloved Dickens modelled in wax hanging up in Miss Frost's shop. It was mounted on a background of blue in a circular black frame. Could he but succeed in obtaining it, a load would be taken off his mind, and the problem of what to buy Walter for a Christmas present would be at once removed. As he gazed with longing eyes towards the coveted object, he became positively fidgety to buy it. If the proprietor would part with it, it must become his. Yes, it was for sale, he was told. " How much? " enquired the poet, thinking that such a treasure ought to be procured regardless of cost. Four-and-sixpence was the price demanded. " I'll take it with me now," eagerly replied the poet as he at once closed with the offer.

The eulogies exchanged between the giver and the receiver when the waxen Dickens was produced on Christmas Day, fully repaid the poet for his trouble. Walter was delighted with it. If it had cost its weight in gold it could not have been more appreciated. I sometimes look at it now as a memento of never-to-be-forgotten days!

Whatever Christmas appeals came to Swinburne's notice, none received more prompt attention than that of a certain Society for aiding Seamen. Forgetful and absent-minded as he was about mundane affairs—and he included the operation of filling in cheques among the curses that beset mankind—he never allowed this appeal to escape his memory. In fact, at Christmas it was uppermost in his mind. Whether it was due to a sense of duty or of pleasure I do not pretend to say, but the sending of his contribution to his " Mariners," as he used to call his beneficiaries, never irked him in the least. After he had written his cheque, he would come downstairs and announce to Walter in a pleased and happy voice, " Here's my cheque for the ' Mariners! ' I'm going to send it off now so that it will get there in good time." After Swinburne died this duty devolved on Walter, and although Isabel (Miss Swinburne) would write to remind either Walter or me not to forget "Algernon's Mariners," my husband was always the first to remember it, and however busy he might happen to be, "Algernon's cheque " was always despatched.

Towards December 25th almost every day brought bulky and interesting packages from friends of either Swinburne or Walter. These would often be opened by me, and sometimes the contents proved both surprising and amusing.

The turkey deserves a special notice and a description of this prepossessing bird may divert the reader, for it stands out in the annals of " Turkeydom " as a unique specimen differing from any other of its kind in one unusual particular. It was a veritable plutocrat in appearance and half covered with gold! Shorn of feathers and hanging up in a poulterer's shop in the cold staring immodesty of the " altogether," a turkey is by no means a pleasing or edifying-looking object to the artistic eye, although from a gastronomic point of view it makes quite a different appeal. But the " gilded fowl " that annually came as a present from Lady Leighton Warren—the sister of the poet Lord de Tabley—was a very superior spectacle. When it came it was paraded round the house as a huge joke, and I christened it " Midas." Pinned to its breast were many " orders "—rosettes of ribbon of divers hues, and the head, feet and scaly shanks, and the whole of its long, hideous, fleshy protuberance of mottled red and blue neck were discreetly covered by a thick layer of gold paint.

Lying in state in a box lined with frilled pink and white paper, and decked out with all the finery of festoons of variegated holly and sprigs of mistletoe, the recumbent scion of a noble house looked almost too gorgeous to be eaten.

For the purpose of buying Swinburne's present, Walter and I decided that a final rampage would prove an interesting wind-up to a busy week. We didn't know what to give the poet, and on Christmas Eve when it was growing quite late, we happened to be passing Buszard's in Oxford Street, and seeing a large printed card in the window bearing the inscription " Partridge Pies " we entered the shop and Walter asked for one.

The place resembled a bee-hive, so crowded was it with late shoppers. A harassed-looking assistant came forward and conducted us to a counter where wonderful erections, like miniature haystacks, were on view. We chose a medium-sized one for our joint present to Algernon, and while it was being packed up, Walter walked to another part of the shop and came back to where I was sitting, bearing in his hands a box of crackers. " Who on earth have you bought those for? " I enquired, for I considered crackers quite a ridiculous institution, and never intended buying any. " Not for *you*," he retorted with an amused chuckle, and an accent on the pronoun. " I know you are far too *old* for that sort of thing, so I've bought them for somebody who *will* appreciate them, and you'll see who *that* is —to-morrow !

Our chief concern now was the safe transit of the pie. As it made a heavy parcel, we carried it in turns, and while I was custodian of the crackers, Walter was responsible for the pie and *vice versâ.* In this manner we arrived home, happy and hungry, to find that quite a transformation had been effected during our absence. The house was gay with decorations, and I must say that at The Pines we were not satisfied with half-hearted exhibitions of festivity. There was always a great piece of mistletoe hanging in the hall, and even the staircase and passages were decorated. The " Christmassy " look of the home at this festive season enhanced by holly and mistletoe reaching nearly to the ceiling and adorning every picture frame, delighted the Bard.

Whilst we were dining, a loud peal at the front door-bell resounded along the hall. It surely could not be the " Waits "—the two or three wretched urchins who call themselves " carol singers " would not ring until they had finished afflicting us with " When Shepherds watch their flocks by night," and similar dirges, for dirges they were as tortured by these dreadful small boys. Our surmise was correct; the boys were still singing through the letter-box in their high treble voices, and the maid came in with the announcement that Mr. MacIlvaine's butler had just left a big box with his master's compliments.

CHRISTMAS AT THE PINES

This friend, knowing the predilections of the housemates for anything savouring of Christmas had always endeavoured to make his present appropriate to the occasion. He certainly achieved a *coup* this time. When the box was opened, it revealed a Yule log. It was made of some kind of composition or *papier maché*, and hollowed out so that it could be lighted up inside. I determined to use it as a table decoration on the morrow. This was a happy thought, for Swinburne was charmed with it.

Christmas Day, as is usual in this country of topsy-turvy climatic conditions, was muggy and warmish, instead of the hoped-for cold and frosty morning. This did not please Swinburne at all. He resented any whimsical vagaries on the part of the Clerk of the Weather. He declared at such times he was being cheated out of his rights. What would have pleased him was the scene of the Christmas card of childhood's tradition, a landscape covered with snow, trees clothed in a frosty mantle, icicles hanging from the water-spouts, and all the rest of the paraphernalia of an old-fashioned winter. When it was "blowing great guns" he was happy, and cold weather so exhilarated him that had there been a snowstorm, and he unable to be out in it, he would have suffered like Tantalus.

THE HOME LIFE OF SWINBURNE

It did not, however, really matter to the poet what the weather was on Christmas Day. At the best of times, the Sabbath Day was by no means calculated to make *his* heart rejoice, for on that day he was deprived of his usual walk, and on that account alone he heartily detested it. Wimbledon Common, on week-days so restful and unpopulated, was invariably thronged on Sundays and at holiday times. Swinburne never crossed the threshold then, but remained indoors, a very uneasy victim until the crowds had disappeared and left him free to enjoy his walk in peace and quiet.

With Christmas Day and Boxing Day the prospect of " half a week of Sundays " had to be faced with as much resolution as the poet could muster. So with the characteristic fortitude of a Mark Tapley, he prepared to make the best of it and took credit in being jolly.

The arrival of the postman proved a diversion, and his budget of cards never failed to amuse him. Naturally he got a goodly supply from strangers. What became of these latter, I cannot say. They disappeared—and that is all one knew of them. But cards from relatives and intimate friends adorned his mantlepiece for days. These messages of goodwill always contained some allusion to his two pet subjects—the sea and the children ; and

CHRISTMAS AT THE PINES

Walter responded to Swinburne's gift of a pictured ship by one at the New Year of a pictured baby. It is before me now as I write:

To the Child-lover A. C. S.
From T. Watts-Dunton, New Year's Day, 1906.

On this same occasion a great triumph was secured by the poet's sister, Isabel, who had the happy thought of presenting her brother with a set of reproductions of the ten Bambini by Andrea della Robbia which ornaments the front of the Ospedale degli Innocenti (Foundling Hospital) at Florence.

These quaintly swaddled little boys are not of equal attractiveness, though doubtless all are beautiful examples of skill in modelling. But Swinburne was enthusiastic about them all He had seen the originals in Italy, and as he showed the little pictures one after another, he could not make up his mind which baby bore off the palm for beauty. How small a thing can gladden the heart of a great man, and for the time being the Bambini made him forget it was a sort of Sunday and that there was no going out for him. As it happened, he managed to fill in his day quite comfortably. There were always his books—his solace and his delight—to browse on. Moreover, there were several chapters from "A Christmas Carol" to be rehearsed for the Dickens reading in the evening, and he devoted some time to getting as near word-perfect as possible. As I have mentioned, I was astonished when I first heard him read "Martin Chuzzlewit" to find he did not so much appear to be reading, as speaking a part learned by rote. Walter told me that Swinburne seldom read anything from Dickens without having previously made a careful study of the chapter or chapters before reading them aloud. Here again was an instance of imitation being the sincerest form of flattery. Dickens must have done the same when reading his own works to crowded audiences.

As in most houses, our Christmas dinner was a family affair—a jolly and homely little gathering. Our only guest, outside the circle of relatives, was Mr. Mackenzie Bell, for whom my husband entertained a great regard. For myself, who had only been married a month, it seemed as if some magician's wand had touched me when I found myself presiding at this Dickensian dinner-table. When the table was arranged, looking so pretty with the Yule log in the middle, and little bundles of crackers scattered at intervals over the cloth,

CHRISTMAS AT THE PINES

Swinburne slipped quietly down from his library, and having got the maid to show him where each member of the party was to sit, he placed an addressed envelope by the side of each cover. These contained the Christmas cards (duly inscribed) which he had been at such pains to select. In the performance of this ritual none of us was ever forgotten by the poet.

A chorus of amusing sallies greeted the entrance of the turkey, " done and dished," as we recalled the golden glories of the " noble bird " now guillotined and deprived of most of its splendours.

More fun came at the end when, the repast being over, there was a general pulling of Christmas crackers. Swinburne now appeared to be thoroughly in his element. The fine ceremoniousness with which he bowed across the table to his old friends, Miss Watts and Mrs. Mason, as he requested the honour of a "tug-of-war," was a " sight for sore eyes," and great was the amusement we all derived from hearing the Bard read the doggerel bits from the mottoes. He kept the table in a roar with his witticisms, and eagerly searched his end of the cracker in the hope that it might contain a specimen of cracker poetry. Eventually everybody's mottoes were handed to him to read. This was a divine moment for such an elocutionist. He carefully unrolled each little slip of paper, and in as stirring tones as he could command—and the more stupid the lines the more pathos he contrived to put into his voice— he would " pray silence " for the recital of some absurd morsel. At the conclusion he would cast up the whites of his eyes to the ceiling, and after heaving a tremendous sigh, exclaim, "A sublime line!—a truly poetic line! What would I not give to have written it! " When it came to the turn of Walter's young niece, Miss Aimée Watts —a charming girl hailing from Australia—or myself, Swinburne's eyes sparkled with mischief. He solicited us both in turn to be his cracker partners, and the motto in each case of course contained some rubbish about love. He endeavoured to make the ridiculous verses more ridiculous still, and loud were the laughs when he read with emphasis and affected emotion such amorous stuff as :

> You are so fair that Cupid's dart
> Can ne'er be pulled from my fond heart.

The motto that resulted from his " pull " with me was more ambitious. Swinburne rendered the lines as fervently as though they had come straight from Sappho herself. Here they are :

CHRISTMAS AT THE PINES

O valorous knight, whose eyes are as blue
   As the sky which is calm above tempests that grieve,
My heart is my Christmas present to you,
   So take it and wear it—but not on your sleeve.

"Ah!" he said with the most profound gravity, " that person, whoever he is, *deserves* to be Poet Laureate."

When the guests had departed, the poet had quite thrown over the part of Master of the Revels. He was now the serious Dickensian and read the selected passages from "A Christmas Carol." The peacefulness of the closing hours of the day was in strange contrast to the mirth of the dinner, and I cannot say that I was sorry when the evening came to an end and Swinburne took leave of us with a courteous bow and a cheery "Good-night."

CHAPTER XV

THE SEA AND THE BABIES

NEXT to love of his friends came Swinburne's love of the sea. And next to his love of the sea ranked his love of babies. Admirers of the poet may express some surprise that I do not include his love of books. I purposely avoided that inclusion. Books were his very life. They were as essential to his existence as the food he ate. And just as most people would sicken and die without their daily bread, so would Swinburne have collapsed without his daily books.

Swinburne's love of the sea was the natural emotion of one whose childhood's home was within hearing of its waves. Moreover, in Admiral Swinburne he honoured as sire one who had a distinguished career as a sailor-man. So that both heredity and environment united to invite and continued to strengthen his splendid affection for the sea, expressed in immortal words.

The Bard's love of babies presents a problem which I have always found at once exciting and baffling. It may be that he felt in looking at babies that charm of a profound mystery suggested by the beauty of someone newly arrived on earth. However that may be, the admiration approaching idolatry for the speechless infant which Swinburne professed was not a pose : it was real.

It must be confessed, however, that the poet knew nothing of that type of child whose conduct is summed up in the elastic description " naughty " Had he ever had the dubious privilege of nursing a fractious infant, he might have been tempted to compose a lyric after the manner of Thomas Hood, who voices the sentiments of a parent towards a kicking sleepless brat of the male species in this way :—

> Lullaby, oh, lullaby!
> What the devil makes you cry?

Throughout Swinburne's numerous poems about babies and children one hears nothing of a peevish infant, a spoilt child, a sulky boy or a greedy boy, although he got no end of fun out of, and expressed the greatest admiration for that delightful fictitious youth " the fat boy in Pick-wick." As to the little girl,

> Who wore a little curl
> Right in the middle of her forehead.
> When she was good
> She was very, very good,
> But when she was bad she was horrid,

perhaps in real life at some unlucky moment he had encountered *that* young person, for he declares the angelic temper and sublime qualities of " Little Nell " as too good to be true, and incontinently dubs her " a monster as inhuman as a baby with two heads." But all *his* geese were swans, and he ecstatically speaks of babes, from birth upwards, as :—" adorable, sweet, living, marvellous." In terms of extravagant adulation he praises with bated breath their " dimpling smiles," their " pink toes," their " rosebud hands," their " heavenly eyes," their " flower-soft fists," and so on—*ad nauseam*, a cynic would say. Of a baby " Three weeks old," he sings :

> Three weeks since there was no such rose in being ;
>   Now may eyes made dim with deep delight
> See how fair it is, laugh with love, and seeing
>   Praise the chance that bids us bless the sight.
>
> Three weeks old, and a very rose of roses,
>   Bright and sweet as love is sweet and bright,
> Heaven and earth, till a man's life wanes and closes
>   Show not life or love a lovelier sight.

THE SEA AND THE BABIES

Three weeks past have renewed the rose-bright creature
Day by day with life, and night by night.
Love, though fain of its every faultless feature,
Lends not words to match the silent sight.

It is very lovely, and I for one simply adore all his poems in praise of babies. But if the poet had seen a baby screaming itself purple in the face, he wisely kept it dark. I very much doubt if he ever had witnessed such a spectacle, for people took care that he only saw their babies when on their best behaviour.

I myself know a lady (Frances Forbes-Robertson) who is proud of the fact that Swinburne nursed her in his arms the day she was christened. When she told Walter and myself of this interesting occurrence I was very curious to know how she had behaved on this momentous occasion. She was not able to enlighten me from first-hand evidence of course, but I remember how earnest she appeared to be in hoping that, " for the poet's sake," she had refrained from making an exhibition of herself.

The little infant of the slums was simply an unknown quantity to the Bard, and the bare idea of a dirty baby was not to be entertained for a moment. He always thought one of the funniest things in the electioneering episode in

173

" Pickwick " was the idea of the " twenty *washed* men waiting at the street door to be shaken hands with "—a most delightful touch. He had heard of and possibly seen many a specimen of the great unwashed, but an unwashed baby—never! Truth to tell, his experiences of child-life were confined to the region of " purple and fine linen," and he never went near Famine street for his types. To look even of a picture of a miserably-clad little child would, I think, have made him perfectly wretched, though he translated Hugo's poem about *Les Enfants Pauvres* whom God had sent with wings and *retrouvé avec des haillons*! He loved to think of all babies as well fed and continuously happy and of course smiling. He loved to look at the portraits of fat chubby babies, and I remember how he gloated over an exquisite volume filled with portraits of children and babies entitled *Les portraits de l'enfant* by Moreau Vanthier. I think his cousin, Mrs. Leith, brought it for him one day, and after she went, he called me in to look at it. How he raved over all the babies—wonderful little Dukes and Princesses of a bygone age, some dressed in costly lace robes, whilst others, half clothed, revealed arms and legs as fat as butter! His beau-ideal of a baby was that of Léopold de Medicis as an infant—

the original of which by Tiberio Titi hangs in the Pitti Palace, Florence. Swinburne's small reproduction stood upon his mantelpiece, and he must have gazed at it continually. He pointed out this luscious little specimen to me the day the book arrived, and not even in his extensive vocabulary could he find adjectives sufficiently rich to express his admiration for this little Italian baby. As he bade me look at it, reclining in royal state on a very gorgeous cushion, the little limbs only partially covered by the most exquisite coverlet of embroidered gold and precious stones, his finger travelled lovingly over the fat baby arms and chest. " Oh, the little duck! Did you ever see such darling dimples? Just look at those sweet little arms! Isn't he perfect?" exclaimed this child-worshipper, with a mouth almost watering as he got to the end of his superlatives; and thinking of nothing more expressive to say, he had to resort to " lip-smacking " as a *pis aller*. I verily believe if Swinburne could have seen that baby in the flesh, he would have been tempted to eat him from sheer admiration of his perfections.

Of course his friends were aware of his infatuation, and helped to foster the baby craze. Fond parents literally pelted the poet with photographs of their respective offspring. Not only did his relations send him the latest photo of " the latest," but the relations' relations sent them as well. Swinburne's collection of baby portraits was distinctly large, ranging as it did over a wide field. But he loved the lot. Catholic in taste, he welcomed the arrival of a photo of a baby in long clothes with almost as much ardour as the parents themselves. But he never wrote of his later baby-loves at much length. His " first fine careless rapture " had been expended years before in the affection he lavished upon Walter's little nephew, Bertie Mason. Some of the sweetest lyrics in the world are written in his honour. The following is his portrait :

Here is a rough
   Rude sketch of my friend,
Faint coloured enough
   And unworthily penned.

Fearlessly fair
   And triumphant he stands,
And holds unaware
   Friends' hearts in his hands;

Stalwart and straight
   As an oak that should bring
Forth gallant and great
   Fresh roses in spring .

THE SEA AND THE BABIES

Each action, each motion,
　　Each feature, each limb,
Demands a devotion
　　In honour of him :

Head that the hand
　　Of a god might have blest,
Laid lustrous and bland
　　On the curve of its crest :

Mouth sweeter than cherries,
　　Keen eyes as of Mars,
Browner than berries
　　And brighter than stars.

Nor colour nor wordy
　　Weak song can declare
The stature how sturdy,
　　How stalwart his air.

As a king in his bright
　　Presence chamber may be,
So seems he in height—
　　Twice higher than your knee.

And well though I know it,
　　As fain would I write,
Child, never a poet
　　Could praise you aright.

I bless you? the blessing
　　Were less than a jest
Too poor for expressing;
　　I come to be blest,

THE HOME LIFE OF SWINBURNE

With humble and dutiful
Heart, from above :
Bless me, O my beautiful
Innocent love !

This little hero fully reciprocated his poet friend's tender passion. But the sad fact remains that a few of his infantile acquaintances with whom he sought to ingratiate himself did not take to him. His magnetism did not work quickly with children, and failed with those of whom he saw but little. His hard and futile efforts with some children were enough to make the angels weep. I know on the best authority that his propitiatory antics sometimes met with a very cool reception, the mites being either too bored or too frightened to meet him halfway. With him, it was indeed a case of *un qui aime l'autre qui se laisse aimer*.

Most of the Bard's pictures of infants were gifts ; but a few of them he had purchased. On the table at which I am writing stands a specimen of the latter. It is a miniature figure modelled in some composite material. It represents a new-born babe emerging from an egg-shell. The child is of the tint of terra-cotta and has a very ugly face. Presumably Swinburne saw some beauty in the image or was fascinated by the modelling of its limbs or by its mobility, for the figure

178

is mounted on a wire and wobbles when touched. He was very proud of his purchase and set great store by it. Where he picked it up I do not know; he had acquired the artistic treasure before I made his acquaintance. More than once he called my attention to the tiny work of art and expatiated, sometimes humorously, sometimes seriously on its " points."

Perhaps the most convincing proof that I can adduce of the genuineness of Swinburne's child-worship is this: a flippant comment on a baby indulged in even by a writer so dear to him as Sir Walter Scott caused the Bard to " see red."

In the " Journal of Sir Walter Scott " there occurs under April 10, 1828, this passage :—

> The baby is that species of dough which is called a fine baby. I care not for children till they care a little for me.

In his essay on the " Journal," Swinburne contrasts Scott's " tenderness for a dog with such irreverence towards an infant " and denounces it " as a disgraceful reflection on one of his grandchildren." He dismisses the offence against His Majesty the Baby with the remark: "After all, Scott was neither a Homer nor a Victor Hugo."

When one reflects that no eulogy uttered by Swinburne about Scott appeared to him excessive,

one cannot doubt that he was every inch a
" babyolator " when he thus attacked the author
of " Ivanhoe."

Looking back now, I cannot understand why we
never secured a house or cottage of our own by
the sea—at least for the summer months. The
two friends had never done so during all the long
period of their joint tenancy of The Pines, and it
never occurred to me to acquire a *pied-à-terre* in
any one selected spot. Had I done so, it might
have saved weary tramps in different localities in
search of a furnished house, or part of a house
that the Poet might like. He so adored the sea
that it is natural to wonder why he never acquired
a sea-side abode at one of his favourite places,
especially the Isle of Wight—the beautiful Vectis
of his dreams—or on the coast of his beloved
Northumberland. But Swinburne was not like
other men, and even if he had inherited a property
of his own he would not have known what to do
with it. Walter was everlastingly on the look out
for a suitable place where he could take the Bard
for his summer holiday, and after my marriage I
joined in the hunt and in explorations of
inspection. No pilgrims in search of the Golden
Fleece encountered more drawbacks than fell to
our share in endeavouring to obtain the almost

unobtainable. Walter from long experience knew to a nicety what Swinburne would like, and he had given me such minute directions on the subject that I was considered qualified for the post of "investigator-in-chief." It was so difficult to get the right thing.

The conditions demanded for the Poet's comfort and well-being were manifold. Hardly anything seemed to be just right. I don't know whether it was the house or the place or the bathing that came first in importance, but Swinburne's contentment with all three was absolutely essential. The place had to be secluded and quiet, what the Bard called an " esplanady " place being anathema to us all. The house had to be within easy distance of the sea, and must contain no " lodgers " except the party from The Pines. Above all the Bard insisted on a sandy beach where deep-water bathing was possible at all tides! Walter was often far too busy to look after the preliminaries himself, so I was told off to *orienter* ('as he expressed it), with injunctions to report progress as soon as possible. When I thought I had hit upon an ideal spot complying with all the required conditions as nearly as possible, I would write off excitedly for him to come and inspect my find. He would arrive

in a hopeful mood, fully prepared to praise my
discovery and with no intention of finding flaws.
But gradually his trained eye would discover some
drawback that I had not thought of, and the weary
search would be renewed. Perhaps the house itself
was not just right for Swinburne. Perhaps the
walks around the neighbourhood were too danger-
ous for one who could not be relied upon to hear
and get out of the way of an occasional motor car
passing along the road; or if other things were
right, the bathing might be wrong, for it was of
the utmost importance that Swinburne's bathing
place would permit of his plunging into the water
in puris naturalibus. He, of course, was quite
ignorant of the elaborate plans made for his entertainment, and to do him justice I am sure if he
had known of all the efforts made on his behalf,
he would have been more than sorry to be the
cause of so much labour. He was not fussy, and was
so simple in his tastes and requirements that an
inexperienced person would have thought it quite
an easy matter to select a place that he would like.

I remember soon after my marriage going on a
visit of inspection in the hope of finding the exact
thing, and starting off joyously confident of
success. We selected a small seaside village in
Kent where, during a stay at Margate, I had

espied a little house in an unfrequented by-way, which I considered would be most suitable. The country round about was very charming, and I hastened to inform Walter of the desirability of taking it as being eminently suitable for Swinburne's requirements. He came down to see what I had found and I shall never forget the way in which he entered into minute particulars about everything. Joy! the house was all right. He carefully measured the distance from the house to the shore and pronounced that nearly all right, but alas for my rising hopes, when he came to inspect the beach and saw the sea retiring in the distance, he regretfully announced that the tides would be all wrong for Swinburne's bathing. On this part of the coast the sea would never come up high enough to enable the poet to plunge conveniently into deep water. And the idea of his *walking* through the sea till he reached a swimming depth was not to be considered for a moment. Hence my toil and hope on this occasion were wasted from this cause alone.

Another thing which weighed very considerably was the romantic interest of any part of the coast-line overlooking a part of the sea covering submerged territory. Hence the fascination that Dunwich held for them both. In fact, any part of a coast formed after the sea had swallowed a piece of Old England had on the Bard the effect of a potent and awe-inspiring spell. For this reason the counties of Norfolk and Suffolk were preferred to almost any others. The shelving cliffs of Suffolk inspired Swinburne's magnificent poem " By the North Sea," and it was at Cromer, years before, that part of "A Midsummer Holiday " was written. Curiously enough it was at this latter place that my first visit to the sea accompanied by the poet took place.

For various reasons, chief among them the tremendous climb that a bathe would entail in order to reach the sea owing to the great height of the cliffs at Overstrand, the Mill House, where the two friends had often stayed before, was no longer eligible, though Walter and I paid a visit there together to see if we could somehow make it serve. It grieved us to have to seek other lodgings, for the poet and Walter had been honoured guests, and Mr. Jermy, the miller, and his daughter now gave me hearty welcome also. They tried hard to persuade us, and with a note of regret in his voice, the old miller, now dead, enquired, " What is Mr. Swinburne busy with now? I was looking forward to hearing him read again." I could hardly believe my ears, for it sounded so odd coming from such a quarter. But it was nevertheless genuine, and Walter replied that the poet was very busy indeed preparing his poems for the press. "More proofs then?" hazarded the miller. "Ah, yes, to be sure, more proofs," said Walter with genial alacrity.

It seems that on the poet's previous visits he had been in the habit of reading proofs aloud to his host, and many a summer evening would these two spend together in the garden of the Mill House. Long yarns would the worthy miller spin about Swinburne, telling how in the morning, or after lunch, the inevitable package having arrived for the poet, he would propose reading out some of the poems in the evening, " If Mr. Jermy would be kind enough to listen! " (how characteristic and delightful of the Bard!) " How I looked forward all day long to the evening, when, after my work in the fields or at the mill was over, I should sit down beside him and listen to him. I think he liked reading to me," proudly remarked the old man with a *very* wise shake of the head. Such a confession inwardly entertained me, for it fully confirmed my opinion that Swinburne so appreciated an audience that he positively felt lost without one. We all shook hands at parting, and as I felt the rough horny palm of this son of the soil between my fingers, I came away with the conviction that Swinburne could not have had a better listener. As we stood on the roadside whilst father and daughter waved their farewells from the old white gate, the miller's cheery voice rang out: " Give my best regards and kind remembrances to Mr. Swinburne." These I duly conveyed to the poet when he arrived at Cromer some few days later, and all sorts of messages and good wishes were returned that filled the heart of his old friend, the miller, with joy.

Walter and I made tracks in a westerly direction and engaged rooms on the Runton Road—some distance from the little town of Cromer—where there was a fine stretch of sandy beach, and where the Bard could bathe in utter seclusion. Then he went home to fetch Swinburne and I stayed behind to await their arrival. How well I remember meeting them at the Railway Station a few days afterwards. Swinburne was very gay, and all excitement at again smelling the sea. As we drove to the house, I could not help noticing how really smart he looked. There was something different about him that I had never noticed before, but in the bustle of finding the luggage and getting clear of the station, I could not define just what it was. It was not the overcoat he carried over his arm, exceptional though this was. Then, as he sat opposite to me in the cab, it suddenly dawned upon me that his restless hands were encased in quite a smart pair of tan gloves—how he must have hated them! I was deeply interested in this astounding innovation, and as soon as Walter and I found ourselves alone after arriving at the lodgings, I asked the reason for such an unheard-of proceeding. His face assumed a wistful and tender little smile as he unfolded the story of the gloves. It seems that for this special occasion the poet had surreptitiously unearthed a pair of gloves, and put them in his pocket before leaving home. Much to Walter's astonishment, during the journey he produced them, asking to be reminded to put them on a little time before their arrival at their destination, remarking, " I should not like Clara to meet me at the station without any gloves on."

So, he had put on these uncomfortable gloves solely for me! How this sweet little admission touched me! When Swinburne afterwards joined us at dinner I could only look at him with a renewed feeling of tender regard for such a graceful and naïve act of courtesy.

He was so unmindful of any sort of weather conditions that it was difficult for him to adapt himself to them. In fact he never could do so. He did not readily understand that it might be unwise to go swimming except under favourable conditions with regard to the elements. He was for taking a plunge the day after his arrival, no matter what the weather would be like, and for the purpose of doing so he and Walter went down to explore the beach.

The very sight of the sea seemed to fire this stormy petrel to instant action, and a yearning to strip and plunge headlong into the waves was not to be resisted. A boat had been engaged before his arrival, and about noon he gave orders to the boatman to row him some distance out to sea in order that he could dive from the stern into very deep water. Walter told me what a splendid dive he always gave, but although on this occasion he appeared to enjoy the exercise quite as much as usual, he got into the boat in a very cold and exhausted condition. The sea that he loved so well did not appear to have the same beneficial effect as of yore, and instead of invigorating, it seemed to weaken him. Swinburne put this down to the roughness of the sea, but he did admit that the water was *rather* cold. Not that this first attempt deterred him in the least, although it rendered his companion nervous and apprehensive.

THE SEA AND THE BABIES

The next day found him as eager as ever to test his swimming prowess, with alas, no greater success than before. This second trial did not improve matters. He again emerged from the water white and exhausted, and almost blue with the cold. This condition of affairs became alarming. Swinburne confessed to feeling extremely tired, and it distressed Walter to see him looking so unlike himself. Afterwards he was asked to forgo his swimming altogether—at least for the time being. As it was obviously doing him harm Swinburne reluctantly consented, but not without many pangs and heartaches. It was an intense disappointment to them both. The Bard would roam about the beach, looking seaward with longing eyes. What were his thoughts, I often wondered. To have to deny himself the luxury of swimming in his beloved sea was very cruel. But he bore it bravely, and so enjoyed walking by the shore that the temptation to board the boat was soon cast aside. He would take long walks inland, too, sometimes alone, and often accompanied by Walter and me.

One day we made a sort of bet as to where we would find the greatest number of landslips—in a southerly or northerly direction. Swinburne declared that he had noticed several huge gaps in the cliffs going north, and Walter thought the inroads of the sea had played more havoc with the land southwards. So we first of all went south to observe the effects of a recent landslip that had occurred the year before. Swinburne had no hesitation in agreeing with Walter when he saw a great yawning mountain of earth reaching far away into the sea, and he exclaimed that he had seldom seen a more wonderful and awe-inspiring sight. Both he and I ventured so near to the edge that Walter was in a constant fear that the earth would give way under us and we had repeated peremptory orders to " keep away from the edge for God's sake."

Swinburne admitted that his friend knew far more about the effects of landslips than he or than most people, and all the way home and during dinner interesting talk took place about receding England and submerged towns. I sat at the head of the table listening to it all, and carving the roast duckling which more often than not seemed to be the meat set before me. We all loved it, and if it was a case of *toujours canardeau* it was because we preferred it to any other.

One day I remember this delectable bird did not appear to be as young as it ought to have been, and I experienced some difficulty in carving it. Whilst witnessing my efforts, Walter began telling

THE SEA AND THE BABIES

Swinburne a very amusing story about one of Rossetti's dinner-parties. The Bard loved to hear any sort of anecdote about the poet-painter, and I revelled in the stories they would unfold around " Topsy " (William Morris) and " Gabriel." I was commanded to listen while I wrestled with the anatomy of my recalcitrant bird.

Rossetti, I was told, always persisted in doing the carving himself, though he was by no means a master-hand at the game. His method of carving was as follows : Savagely preparing himself for an onslaught, he would spear the joint or fowl with the carving fork, and go for it with the knife somewhat in the manner of a barbarian trying hurriedly to kill a foe. One night at Cheyne Walk there was a grander dinner party than usual, and a goodly number were sitting at the feast. For the occasion Rossetti had ordered two ducks to be placed on the dish at the same time. He began attacking a bird in his accustomed manner, jerking both ducks from side to side in the dish and incidentally splashing everybody within range with gravy. One of the birds being of grandmotherly toughness, his endeavours to dissect its limbs resulted in his depositing the whole of the other bird on the knees of George Augustus Sala, who was sitting sedately by the

side of his host in full and blameless evening-dress.
Gabriel paused in his work, and discovering where
he had landed the other duck, he stared at his
astonished guest, and quite unabashed by the
mishap calmly drawled—" I say, Sala, just hand
me back that duck."

Swinburne's fondness for making up nonsense
rhymes never wholly left him, and his wonderful
memory enabled him to recall some of the trifles
that either he or Rossetti had scribbled in
" honour " of their mutual friends. I know that
Rossetti has been credited with the amusing
limerick written around Dr. Franz Hueffer, the
accomplished son-in-law of Ford Madox Brown,
but I fancy the Bard had some hand in its compila-
tion—he was then seeing much of Rossetti, and
the pair were in the habit of concocting this form
of jingle together. Walter's story of Rossetti and
the duck set the ball rolling about old times, and
this limerick was spouted anew for my benefit.
Both Swinburne and Rossetti were very friendly
with Dr. Hueffer, who besides being a great
scholar and man of scientific learning, was an
accomplished musician to whom England is
indebted for his championship of the music of
Wagner. As an exponent of Schopenhauer,
however, he was dogmatic and emphatic, and this

unton

To my best & dearest friend I dedicate the first collected edition of my poems: & to him I address what I have to say on the occasion

x

x x x x x x

It is nothing to me that what I write should find immediate or general acceptance: it is much to know that ~~for the world~~ it has ~~enjoyed~~ upon for me the right to address this dedication 'inscribe to this' ~~~~ to you.

Algernon Charles Swinburne

The first and ast sentences from he draft of the Dedicatory Epistle in his collected works.

cult not being to the taste of his jovial friends, they " served him up " the following doggerel, which, it may be added, very much amused Hueffer himself :

> There's a metaphysician called Hueffer
> A hypochondriacal buffer,
>> To proclaim Schopenhauer,
>> From the top of a tower,
> Is the ultimate mission of Hueffer.

I have given it as I remember hearing it : there exists another version.

As was their wont, my husband and Swinburne had brought bundles of MSS., reams of foolscap and books galore to beguile the time during their sojourn by the sea. Swinburne had brought the proofs of certain of his poems for the " Collected Edition," and the dedicatory epistle in prose which he had written for it. He suggested reading it to me—another instance of his innate courtesy, for he knew how much it would please me. This long essay, filling twenty-nine pages of Vol. I of his collected poems, stands out as a piece of masterly prose and reveals Swinburne at his best in scholarship. He introduced the opening sentence with a reminder :—" This is for Walter, you know," and proceeded to read, ever on the look-out for some mistake in the text. If so much as a comma

Clara Watts-Dunton

The waves are a joy to the seamew, the meads to the herd,
And a joy to the heart is a goal that it may not reach.

Algernon Charles Swinburne

Facsimile of Swinburne's inscription in the set of his collected works presented by him to Clara Watts-Dunton.

was omitted or wrongfully introduced, down would go his pencil on the offending line, and his vituperative comments were somewhat of a relief from the strain of following his magnificent prose. As he read on, I was awed by the burning intensity of his language. Two sentences in particular made me very uncomfortable as Swinburne stressed each insulting or bitter word, making me feel the sting of the old saying : " If the cap fits, wear it." His eyes seemed to pierce me through and through as I listened :

The half-brained creature to whom books are other than living things may see with the eyes of a bat and draw with the fingers of a mole his dullard's distinction between books and life : those who live the fuller life of a higher animal than he know that books are to poets as much part of that life as pictures are to painters or as music is to musicians, dead matter though they may be to the spiritually still-born children of dirt and dullness who find it possible and natural to live while dead in heart and brain.

Marlowe and Shakespeare, Æschylus and Sappho, do not for us live only on the dusty shelves of libraries.

The concluding sentence, which gave me visions of the unexplored dusty top shelves in the library at home, made me so unspeakably wretched that at the conclusion of the reading I went almost weeping to Walter to receive his assurance that Swinburne did *not* mean me. Well, however,

THE SEA AND THE BABIES

was I rewarded for my suffering. When the
volumes appeared the Bard gave me the whole set
for a birthday present, and inscribed them to me,
enriching the fly-leaf with the following lines :

The waves are a joy to the seamew, the meads to the herd,
And a joy to the heart is a goal that it may not reach.

The book on the tapis at this time, I well
remember, was " The Woman in White." The
pitch of enthusiasm to which Swinburne worked
himself whilst reading it to Walter was unforget-
table. He became short of breath at the thrilling
situations. The characters gripped his imagination
to such an extent that for the time being he lived
inside the parts created by the novelist. I had
not been present at the beginning of the narrative,
so I only heard it fragmentarily. The story was
not being read for the first or even the second
time. Its present innings had started at Putney,
and Swinburne had taken care not to leave
it behind. Just before sitting down to dinner one
evening, the Bard—having concluded a wonderfully exciting chapter—held up his glass of beer,
and just as he might have been toasting an absent
friend exclaimed, alluding to Fosco who drinks the
health of Miss Halcombe, " And well might he
drink her health ! So do I."

CHAPTER XVI

TABLE TALK

FORTUNATELY for his guests, before he came to live with Walter at The Pines, Swinburne rarely made any attempt at hospitality beneath his own bachelor roof in Great James Street. He was in the habit of lunching or dining with Walter, when they were neighbours in Great James Street, either at the Cock Tavern in Fleet Street or at the London Restaurant at the corner of Chancery Lane.

The very idea of the Bard grappling with the intricacies of a *cuisine*, especially under the auspices of a " laundress " (that is, I fancy, the correct name for the female who " does," in more ways than one, for her lodgers) makes me laugh—or weep. With the assistance of the egregious " Mrs. Crupp," David Copperfield *did* have the forethought to order a well-chosen menu from the

198

pastrycook's on the occasion of his little dinner at his chambers in Buckingham Street.

Would that Swinburne had done likewise when he invited Justin Huntly MacCarthy to lunch with him. A day or two before this festivity the Bard had met this extremely nice young man at a private view of the Blake Exhibition. Wishing to show him hospitality, Swinburne with great cordiality exclaimed, " Come to lunch," and forthwith appointed a day. Delighted and honoured by the invitation, the guest duly presented himself and was ushered into the sitting-room where Swinburne was waiting for him. On a table were a few plates, a tin of biscuits, a pot of jam, a bottle of hock—and nothing else. The guest, thinking that the poet's " laundress " would shortly appear bearing at least a dish of cold meat to augment the repast, listened enraptured to his host's conversation and politely awaited his invitation to take his seat at the board. No hospitable female appeared, however, and after a short time, Swinburne, waving his hand towards the jam and the hock, airily said, " Shall we have luncheon now? " and proceeded to place himself before the tin of biscuits and hand the pot of jam to his guest, inviting him to " help himself " He then placed the biscuits within his guest's reach and poured out two glasses of hock.

This weird luncheon proceeded until they had both satisfied themselves with the two solitary comestibles, and emptied the bottle of hock.

Mrs. Disney Leith, in her recollections of her famous cousin, prints a letter from Swinburne to his mother. This letter is written from The Pines and contains this passage : " What stuff people talk about youth being the happiest time of life! Thank God   I am very much more than twice as happy now as I was when half my present age."

An assured and undisturbed happiness in his environment, his pursuits, his intercourse, was the dominant note of his life at Putney Hill. And there was no period of the day when that conscious joy in existence was more manifest than during meal times. For if the poet was a master of monologue, he was by no means incapable of the delightful small talk, the conversational give-and-take, the apt allusions, the appropriate quip. In this unstudied converse he " was quick at the up-take." Meal time was never a dull interlude in the day's duties and distractions.

His manners at the table were of the old courtly school and were charming. He would never think of helping himself until he was quite sure that you had everything you wanted. The salt or the mustard he would pass to you with a little smiling bow and an air of genuine courtliness. He was punctilious over the small observances of the table. For instance, it would never occur to him, at the end of the repast, to throw his napkin down in an untidy heap for a servant to collect and adjust. It was the hero, so to speak, of quite a little ceremony. The rolling-up of it seemed to afford him a real pleasure. He would fold the ends together and smooth out the creases with religious solicitude before slipping it back into its ring. And should the folding and rolling fail to come up to his idea of artistic perfection, he would undo the work of his hands and perform the ceremony all over again. When he was really sure that all the requirements of the case had been met, he would look up at us with a happy, boyish smile and a satisfied ejaculation of " Ah! " as if he had accomplished some difficult feat.

Comment having been made on the remarkable thoroughness with which he conducted this performance, he explained that when he was a little boy in the nursery his mother had taught him to be particular in this matter, and that he still took a pride in following her instructions.

Talking of napkin-rings reminds me of a little

incident. My husband on one occasion gave the poet a celluloid ring, and he explained to me while purchasing it, " I will give this to Algernon for a lark—he will think it is ivory." It cost, I think, a shilling or eighteen pence, and the inexperienced eye would suppose it was real ivory. I doubt if Swinburne had ever heard of celluloid. A little oblong picture of French design was let into the surface of the ring. This decoration had the effect of an exquisite miniature by some artist of the Watteau school, giving an air of expensiveness to what was merely pretty.

When my husband gave his little present to Swinburne, the latter waxed quite eloquent, " Beautiful! " " Charming! " were among his fervent exclamations of delight and appreciation. When he was told what the napkin-ring had cost, he found it difficult to believe it. He shrugged his shoulders and ejaculated repeatedly " Tiens! Tiens! How can such things be? "

When in the mood, he would notice and comment on any trifle on the table, and anything new or pretty immediately arrested his attention. For example he never tired of commenting on a little Queen Anne mustard-pot I had bought. When he had recourse to it, he would gaze on it with an expression of the utmost satisfaction. Its quaint shape and fluted pattern appealed to his artistic sense. "I like this little thing, it is so pretty," he would say as a sort of apology for lingering over its qualities instead of taking his mustard and getting on with his meal. There was one table decoration which he could not stand. He hated to see cut flowers used for ornamentation or indeed for any other purpose. He had an idea that it hurt the poor things to cut them. He described them as innocents who had undergone execution, beautiful heads that had been guillotined, severed from their fair fragile bodies and consigned to the sawdusty basket of M. Sanson. To him flowers presented a tragic spectacle unless they were "all a-blowing and a-growing."

Apropos this peculiar and rather pathetic trait, another incident comes back to me. One springtime I had been into the country and I came upon a wood wherein blue-bells were spread like a carpet. Had I been a poet, the scene would doubtless have conjured up to my mind's eye many exquisite ideas. But I could only think of one, of unseen fairies dancing between the lovely bells, their tread leaving every flower undisturbed. I felt like a female Gulliver in a lovelier Lilliput. From sheer *joie de vivre* I took off my shoes, meaning to join in the revels of the fairy host.

Then something stopped me. I shrank from the idea of trampling like a giant among such exquisite and fragile things. I put on my shoes again. On my return I told Swinburne of my experience, describing the beauty of the scene, the suddenness of the temptation, the equally sudden revulsion of feeling, and I saw that the poet was really moved by my idea.

" It was better not; you might have hurt them," he said.

I do not wish it to be inferred that our table-talk was solely concerned with " trifles light as air." Some chance allusion to French affairs would, perhaps, bring up the name of Napoleon III, the *Napoléon le Petit* of Victor Hugo. This roused the poet to alternate rage and rapture, for he regarded the Emperor as one of the most odious and contemptible of throned criminals, while he worshipped Hugo as the greatest of the literary immortals. To describe his outbursts on these topics as picturesque, passionate, and perfervid is to do them very much less than justice. The atmosphere of the room became electrical, and sparks seemed to crackle in all directions.

When Hugo was the theme, there was no conversation : Swinburne declaimed and we listened. I remember, however, a notable exception to this rule. One day at table he was unusually quiet. He was looking dull and despondent. I asked my husband if Algernon would like to hear me recite a poem I had learned at school. Upon being assured that the poet would be delighted to listen to me, I went over to him and knelt on the floor by his side. I told him that I knew a little poem by Victor Hugo. At the mere mention of " The Master " his unhappy mood passed, like a mist dispelled by the effulgence of the sun. His face became radiant, his attitude that of eager attention. The poem was addressed to a *jeune fille*. The composition was tame and *convenable* to the last degree. But in the eyes of his English singing brother, Victor Hugo was sacrosanct. He fairly beamed on me as I proceeded, and when I had finished he thanked me in his polite way and assured me that I had afforded him great pleasure. His melancholy mood had entirely disappeared, and he began to talk of the days when he " was a kid at Eton."

There was naturally much literary talk at our table. Walter was anxious that I should be qualified to take part in it when the topics were within my intellectual range. There came an occasion when he suggested to me that I might find Border Minstrelsy an interesting field of study. It was a topic frequently trotted out by the housemates at The Pines. I bought a copy of " Border Ballads " and soon discovered as much fascination in " Clerk Saunders " and " The Wife of Usher's Well " as any literary husband could hope for or desire.

There are two stanzas in " Clerk Saunders " which Walter and the Bard delighted to recite alternately. My husband would begin :

> Is there ony room at your head, Saunders?
> Is there ony room at your feet?
> Is there ony room at your side, Saunders?
> Where fain, fain, I wad sleep?

Well I can recall the pleasure Swinburne derived in replying :

> There's nae room at my head, Marg'ret
> There's nae room at my feet;
> My bed it is full lowly now,
> Amang the hungry worms I sleep.

It was weird, but beautiful in a way, and I felt as greatly moved in listening as Swinburne obviously was in reciting.

On the subject of Swinburne and the Border Ballads I received from Lady Archibald Campbell a very interesting letter which I have great pleasure in reproducing here :

Coombe Hill Farm,
Kingston-on-Thames,
September 27th, 1919.

My dear Clara

As you tell me you are writing a monograph of Swinburne (and no one is more fitted to do it than yourself), it has struck me some little incidents might interest you which occurred in the early days of our friendship with him and your husband, when they came together to see us. Of course you know that our friendship with your wonderful " Bird " * began when he was seeing much of Rossetti. But of course we knew him before he had met either the poet-painter or Swinburne.

It was a friend of the Duke and Duchess of Sutherland who brought him to see us. She had often told me what a wonderful man he was. She had made his acquaintance at Rossetti's. Afterwards when he and Swinburne became friends I remember one of my first ventures to please him was half-reciting—half-singing—some of the old Border Ballads. He listened with rapt attention, and with that fascinating politeness of his remarked, " Walter had not told me you had the art of expressing the life of the matchless Scottish Ballads! I in a small way have attempted that form of Ballad myself." I remember his pleasure over " The Twa Corbies"—how he bent his ear near to the piano the better to hear every word; and how " Lord Randal " delighted him—especially about the poisonous eels—when his Mother asks him:

" Where gat ye your dinner, Lord Randal, my son?
Where gat ye your dinner, my handsome young man?"
" I gat eels boil'd in broo; mother, make my bed soon,
For I'm weary wi' hunting, and fain wald lie doon."

Lord Randal's reply saying he dined off " eels boiled in broo "—presumably *poisoned by his " true love "*—delighted him, and how he laughed!

* One of the three pet names for Walter,

THE HOME LIFE OF SWINBURNE

Here is the couplet :—

" O I fear ye are poison'd, Lord Randal, my son !
    O I fear ye are poison'd, my handsome young man !"
" O yes ! I am poison'd ; mother, make my bed soon,
    For I'm sick at the heart, and I fain wald lie doon."

Their adorable simplicity in everyday life *riveted me*, and many other countless memories they call up, which make my heart too full to speak of otherwise than as radiant beacons in my life, which threatened at one time to become for me a slough of Philistine darkness, oppression and repression—certainly a curious combination !

Of course you are coming on Monday, so until then, Au revoir.

Affectionately yours,
JANEY S. CAMPBELL.

On the wall at the left-hand side of the dining-room door at The Pines there hung—and still hangs—a water-colour painting by Miss Elizabeth E. Siddal, who became the wife of Dante Gabriel Rossetti. It is dated 1856. It represents an episode described in the border ballad of " Sir Patrick Spens." Sometimes when Swinburne left the table after lunch, he would stop for a moment to look at this little drawing. It linked him with the past. It has often occurred to me that his first ballads in the archaic style of the Border Minstrelsy were written shortly after Miss Siddal finished her picture. He was, as is well known, an enthusiastic friend of Rossetti.

208

CHAPTER XVII

A WELCOME VISITOR

VISITORS at The Pines were usually impressed by Swinburne's affability and courtesy, but in the majority of cases they made very little impression on him. One notable exception is worth a small chapter.

The welcome visitor was Marion Crawford the novelist, whose writings Swinburne much esteemed. The visit came about in this way. Walter had written to Mr. Crawford telling him how A. C. S. and he had been enthralled while reading "A Cigarette Maker's Romance." The letter ended like this, " When you are in England we should much like to meet you." Crawford was evidently pleased, and when he next came to this country, one of his first visits was to The Pines.

I can still recall vividly the occasion on which he came to us. It was a splendid day in mid-June, about four o'clock, and he was shown into the dining-room which overlooks the garden, at that time a glowing perspective of flower and foliage. When I entered the room, our guest's back was turned towards me. He was standing at the window admiring the scene. He turned quickly as he heard me enter. My first impression was that he looked very much of a man. He stood well over six feet, and his figure was in the nicest proportion to his height. He was bronzed, and his hands were beautifully shaped. What struck me most about him was the very bright blue of his eyes. So bright was the blue that I found it hard to believe what I heard subsequently from one who knew him well, that the blue never was so brilliant as when he was on his beloved sea sailing his yacht "Aeda." This was his ruling passion. He was more proud of having himself sailed the "Aeda" from New York to Sorrento than he was of the success of his most popular work. As I looked at him, the thought flashed through my mind that Marion Crawford looked more like the hero of a novel than the writer of one.

Our greeting was cordial. I at once felt myself at ease with him. Having exchanged polite commonplaces, Mr. Crawford expressed his admiration for the garden on which he had just been gazing. "Why," he said with his bewitching smile, "you seem to be in the very heart of the country here, and yet in the front of your house you are in the midst of traffic and the hoots of the motor horns." We talked together for some time before my husband appeared. The pleasure of both men on becoming acquainted was too genuine for any disguise, but Walter had in the drawing-room a business man whom he was bound to rejoin, so it fell to my lot to pilot the visitor to Swinburne's sanctum.

The poet had been told of Marion Crawford's arrival, and never was introduction more easily effected. I cannot recall how the introduction was phrased, and I am inclined to think that there was no formality, but that the men just met and shook hands after the manner of old friends who had not seen each other for a long time. Of course they had many tastes in common. Both loved Italy. Both loved the sea, and each of them had a sincere admiration for the literary output of the other. It was a delightful conversation, especially as Swinburne had not the slightest difficulty in hearing what Crawford said. A pleasant change, this, from the boredom he so often experienced when a visitor's voice failed to "carry." On this occasion, both visitor and host seemed to generate an atmosphere of harmony and repose. So "enthused" did Swinburne become, that while discussing Italy, he dropped into the language of that delightful land. But as his acquaintance with the language was that of a reader and not a speaker, he soon dropped out of it again, notwithstanding Crawford's tactful compliment on his fluency. The deviation into Italian happened when the two men were discussing the "Orlando Furioso" of Ariosto which Swinburne had taken down from his shelves. I confess that a good deal of this part of the talk was a little beyond me; but I shall always recall with gratitude the gallant efforts of our visitor to keep me participating easily in it. When conversation veered round to the sea Mr. Crawford's kind wish for me to join in it was less difficult to comply with, for I, also, loved the sea.

Crawford at last expressed an eager desire to hear Swinburne read one of his own works. And, nothing loth, the Bard read aloud the completed part of "The Duke of Gandia." The novelist appeared greatly impressed. Our visitor stayed with us the whole afternoon, for it was close on dinner-time when he rose to leave When the visit was at an end, and the two men bade good-bye to each other with many hopes expressed for another meeting, I left the poet's library with

A WELCOME VISITOR

Mr. Crawford. As the door of the sanctum closed, he said to me, " I shall never forget this day." He turned and looked at the shut door and said, " It has been wonderful! wonderful! " In silence he came down; and as he said " Good-bye," neither of us imagined the good-bye was said for the last time. By a coincidence these two great men of letters died within twenty-four hours of each other, Crawford on the 9th of April, 1909, Swinburne on the 10th. I have two letters which bring back very vividly that day in June. The first is from Swinburne to Marion Crawford. The two men, so greatly attracted one to the other, naturally engaged in correspondence. The receipt of a letter from the novelist was always regarded by the poet as a specially interesting event, and it made him happy for the whole day. Here is the letter of A. C. S.:

The Pines,
September 4th, 1907.

Dear Mr. Crawford,

Many thanks for Richepin's book. I am quite inclined to believe in the fidelity and accuracy of his Borgian Study. The authorities I never believe in are such " Tedeschi " as " Gregorovius the unreadable "—I would as soon put my faith in " Mommsen " or " Freeman."

What a singularly original and touching story is the *Histoire de l'autre monde!* But, indeed, as much might be said for the other two. I need not say how gratified I

213

am by your recollection of my unfinished play. I am about to publish what is written of it as " The Tragedy of the Duke of Gandia."

With all good greetings from Watts-Dunton.

Very truly yours,

A. C. SWINBURNE.

Mrs. Watts-Dunton is especially delighted with the admirable portraits you sent her, and is writing to you to say so.

It is, perhaps, unnecessary to explain the allusions in the above letter. " Tedeschi " is simply the Italian for Germans. Swinburne who had no love for the Germans as a people, hated both Gregorovius and Mommsen with a perfect hatred. What his grudge against poor Freeman may have been I do not know, but him also he regarded with great dislike. The book by Jean Richepin that occasioned the communication is doubtless *Les Débuts de César Borgia*, the second chapter of which is entitled *Le Cadavre du duc de Gandie*.

The other letter is one written by Marion Crawford to me from Italy a few months after his visit to us:

S. Agnello di Sorrento (Napoli)

Torre San Nicola,

San Nicola Arcella,

Provincia di Cosenza,

Sept. 12th, 1907.

DEAR MRS. WATTS-DUNTON,

Many thanks for your kind and welcome letter, and

A WELCOME VISITOR

for the Book Monthly, when it comes. It ought to come dawdling along a couple of days after the letter itself, but this is an out-of-the-way place. I wish you could see it. Walls eighteen feet thick, sea, rocks, more sea and more rocks, and no habitation visible except a haunted house below, near the beach, and the big half-ruined building on the hill where my farmer lives.

I cannot tell you how much I value your husband's high opinion of " The Cigarette Maker," nor how grateful I am for his open praise of it. I wish I had written twenty better, but there is hardly one I think so good. Mr. Swinburne told me he liked the " Roman Singer "—it must be our Italy that appealed to him, for he loves it as well as I do, and has written undying words about it, which I never shall.

May I ask you a question—" on the sly," as you put it? Or even two? The first is this. In a very unscholarly way, I am very fond of the Greek poets, and I potter amongst the gardens of the Anthology on my own account. I found lately a very beautiful Epitaph of four lines, by an unknown author, " On a friend." Do you think that by any diplomacy it would be possible to bring it to Mr. Swinburne's notice, in the bare hope that he might do it into his matchless English, for all men and for all time? If you think so, I will copy the lines and send them to you. No one, living or dead, ever turned Greek into English as he does here and there through his poems. I do not believe he even knows that scholars have picked out gems here and there and have printed them as his, in their notes.

The other question is, can Mr. Watts-Dunton let me have the sheets of " The Tragedy of the Duke of Gandia " a little early, in order that I may write a review of it in one of the big English Reviews? I think I might do it—not as it deserves—but as well as a professional reviewer, and it would be a labour of love.

Forgive this long letter, I am glad you like the photograph—yes, Mr. Swinburne wrote that you had received it and were pleased.

I leave here on the 15th for my real home, and shall be there off and on all the winter.

With warm greetings to your husband, and sincerest thanks to Mr. Swinburne for his interesting letter about the " Tedeschi " and " Gregorovius the unreadable."

Most sincerely yours,

MARION CRAWFORD.

CHAPTER XVIII

MISCELLANEA

ABOUT anything of a mechanical nature Swinburne had the most primitive ideas. He could poke a fire—after a fashion; and, as we have seen, he could light his candles—after another fashion. But he regarded all machinery as belonging to a world outside his ken. This inability to understand enhanced the awe and admiration with which he regarded the simple contrivances intended to add to the ease of everyday life. His intelligence was so confined to poetry and imaginative literature that even the mechanism of a soda-water syphon was beyond him. When for the first time I manipulated one in his presence, he gazed fixedly at me, evincing considerable apprehension for my safety. I succeeded in releasing a gentle stream into my glass. When I stopped, he said with an accent of admiration and surprise, " How cleverly you did that; I couldn't have done it." I could disclaim the compliment, but I could not truthfully contradict the second part of his comment. I have seen him approach a refractory window-sash with the reluctance of one about to grasp a bunch of nettles, but if the sash remained obstinate under his treatment he would hurl at it a dazzling selection of epithets in at least three different languages. It was a liberal education in swear-words to hear him. I tried to catch the phrases as they dropped in quick succession from his lips; but knowing only English and French, most of his angry eloquence was lost to me. Some of it was no doubt imprecation in the purest Attic Greek.

Foremost among the mechanical arts of which he approved was photography. He spoke enthusiastically of its results and pronounced them " tremendously clever " He raved eulogistically over some snapshots of children done by a cousin of his. The meaning of the phrase, " You touch the button, we do the rest," would have floored him utterly, for he regarded the little pictures almost as works of art.

Although I have seen Walter scores of times with a pad before him writing his own letters, he more often than not dictated them. He was never slow to employ any mechanical device which he thought would make life easier. In his enthusiasm for science he was eager for experiments. Not so the Bard—in this he was Walter's exact opposite. *He* never enquired the why and the wherefore of such things, or whence and by whom came any invention. I believe Swinburne resented even a business letter that was type-written, whereas Walter welcomed the machine-made epistle as affording him relief from deciphering the sometimes awful writing of his correspondents. Under the impression that such a method as typewriting would, with practice, enable him at least to write his own letters, he was eager to purchase one of the numerous machines on the market. We wrote to several companies and for weeks we were deluged with correspondence, descriptive catalogues—and machines. I had learnt to type on a hired machine in anticipation of the day when we should acquire one of our own, and in order that I should be able in turn to teach Walter.

Never shall I forget the arrival of those type-writers! Their escorts from the different companies would leave them at The Pines for a week or more on trial. At one time we had four of them simultaneously in the house. Poor Walter was worried to death between the lot of them, not knowing which to choose, and with each agent praising his own wares. The man from " Remington's" and the " Smith Premier" man would meet in the hall and glare fiercely at each other one day, whilst on another, the Hammond " agent would barge into the " Blick " or the " Yost " clerk as he entered or departed with his own particular machine. Eventually one was selected, and Walter began his lessons in peace and comfort.

What fun we had in the evenings! He proved quite an apt pupil, and when he didn't forget to " shift the key " or strike the lever that produces the spacing, or make some other minor fault, his progress was satisfactory, if slow. I was beginning to feel quite proud of my pupil, and one day when we went to Onslow Square to visit Algernon's sister Isabel, I carried a specimen of Walter's best and latest effort with me. She thought it wonderful ; and turning to me with an eager smile on her charming face, she exclaimed excitedly, " Oh, Clara, if you would but teach dear Algernon how to type, how delightful *that* would be ! " The incongruity of such an idea had the effect of making Walter and me almost double up with laughter. But Isabel, thinking, no doubt, that this contrivance had come as a boon and a blessing to relieve her brother from the tiresome effort of wielding a pen, was oblivious of the fact that Algernon would not and could not be taught.

In his ineptitude with regard to mechanics Swinburne was untrue to the doctrine of heredity. His immediate forbears found a great attraction in them. On this point I may quote an observation made by my husband.

In dealing with the poet's little book on Dickens he says, "It is interesting to remark that Swinburne's father, Admiral Swinburne, was in his own way almost as remarkable as his grandfather. His ability showed itself in a direction in which the poet was strangely deficient—mechanics. He spent much of his time in his carpenter's workshop. He invented more than one mechanical device for which he ought to have taken out a patent. I myself possess one of these devices given me by Lady Mary Gordon. It has always been a special wonder to visitors to The Pines."

Far from being astonished at A. C. S.'s lack of mechanical knowledge, I am disposed to wonder how a man who added so many treasures to English literature managed to get through so much general reading as he did. Barring scientific works, he could read pretty nearly anything, from poetry, history and

philosophy down to " Yellowbacks " and lime-
ricks. And he usually found something to admire
in them all—and often something to abominate.
He was, I remember, extremely fond of Thackeray.
" The Newcomes " was one of his favourite novels,
and Ethel Newcome was his favourite heroine in
fiction. Ethel, I have always thought, must have
appealed to him as resembling some member of his
own family, perhaps one of his sisters.

He never wearied of discussing his favourite
novels, and dwelt with pathetic insistence on the
peculiarities of the various characters. He was
as zealous as an evangelist in his endeavour to
secure converts to his literary beliefs. He tried
to convert me—sometimes with success. He
introduced me to Jane Austen's " Emma "—the
characters in that book being to him living and
faithful friends.

When I had finished reading " Emma " he put
me through quite an examination on the book.
His every question began with " Do you
remember? " or, " I know you have forgotten."
He was delighted that I had noticed how fussy
Mr. Wodehouse became about the way in which
his gruel was prepared, and asked me if I would
have taken the same pains as Emma in order to
meet her father's taste in it. He had a fervent

and almost affectionate appreciation for the work of Jane Austen, and was fond of picturing the England she knew through her eyes. Often I heard him exclaim when referring to " Emma " :
" What a queer little England it must have been then, to be sure ' "

Swinburne knew no German, nor do I remember having seen a German book on his shelves. He disliked the Teuton, and entertained no exalted opinion of his literature. His passionate love of France and of everything French was attributable, I imagine, to the fact that Victor Hugo was a Frenchman.

With Hugo he had a very voluminous correspondence, and he kept a large number of his letters. These I was asked to translate into English. The task was not an easy one, owing to the characteristically literary handwriting of the Master.

When talking about Hugo, the Bard would often lapse into French, and although he had never stayed long in France, he spoke it with a true Parisian accent, and with the ease of one talking in his mother tongue. His achievements in French prose and poetry are convincing proofs of his mastery of that language.

Believing that biography should not avoid the

amusing simply because the smiles evoked are at its subject's expense, I give the following story, for which I am indebted to Mrs. Alys Eyre Macklin who had it direct from her friend Tola Dorian. When Swinburne and my husband visited Paris in November, 1882, to witness the performance of Hugo's *Le Roi s'amuse*, it was arranged that they should meet the great Frenchman at a dinner at his house. Tola Dorian was an almost daily visitor there, and being Swinburne's translator and friend, she was asked to be hostess on the great occasion. This is how she described the meeting :

" It was a cold, dreary day, and poor Hugo was feeling very irritable and nervous, full of aches and pains, more than usually deaf, and in one of his worst moods. It was pitiful to see how he struggled with his weakness; he was like a lion in a net. I told them not to bring the visitors straight in to him, feeling I had better see them first to explain that their host was not in a normal frame of mind, but when Swinburne arrived alone, I saw that he also was in a highly nervous condition.

" ' Watts was not able to come,' he burst out excitedly. ' He has toothache. The poor fellow is suffering agonies. I ought never to have left him. I must get back as soon as possible.

STATUETTE OF VICTOR HUGO

"Now, Swinburne also was deaf, and I shall never forget the scene that followed. Trembling with agitation, he went off into what sounded like a carefully prepared speech full of Eastern hyperbole : Victor Hugo was the great sun round which the little stars, etc., etc., etc. Hugo sat with his head bent forward, his hand to his ear, and his efforts to catch the words gave his face a threatening expression, and his terse 'What does he say? What does he say?' sounded like a growl. This did nothing to tranquillise Swinburne, who grew more and more nervous as he began at the beginning again.

"The result was the same, and I had to come to the rescue as interpreter.

"Had it not been so pathetic, it would all have been intensely funny. All through the meal I had to continue to act as interpreter, and at intervals Swinburne kept on saying to me in an undertone, 'I ought never to have left him. All alone in the hotel—and the poor fellow was suffering agonies!' The climax came when, at dessert, Victor Hugo drank the health of his guest, and Swinburne, raising his glass to toast the 'great master,' in homage, threw the empty glass over his shoulder.

"Victor Hugo did not grasp the full meaning

of the action, and he only stared at the shattered fragments. A kind of childish avarice had developed in him with advancing years, and this got the upper hand of him as he muttered : 'And one of the best glasses too! One of the best glasses!' And that was his refrain long after the poet had left.''

A funny story may be too good to lose, but I should not like the readers of this one to regard it as any sort of anti-climax to the sincere and glowing praise which Hugo bestowed on " *le premier poète anglais actuel* " who touched the " *deux cimes* " of lyric verse and tragic drama.

In order to complete his book " The Age of Shakespeare," Swinburne wished to see a copy of two plays by William Rowley "All's Lost by Lust " and "A New Wonder : a Woman Never Vext." So one day the Bard, Walter and I started off for the British Museum. The way was made smooth for us by a letter written beforehand to the late Mr. Fortescue.

When we arrived at the famous library, we were met by Mr. Fortescue and conducted through a private door into a very secluded little library. Sitting working at a table in this apartment was a tall, white-bearded and strikingly handsome man who flashed a keen glance at Swinburne when we entered.

When the official brought Swinburne his precious Rowley, he directed the poet to a seat near that of the venerable student whom I have described. Once absorbed in his Rowley, Swinburne had eyes for naught else, so my husband and I left him to his labours and went for a stroll through the galleries of the Museum. When we were fairly out of earshot Walter confided to me that Swinburne's good-looking old *vis-à-vis* was Dr. Furnivall, the eminent Shakespearean scholar, with whom, years before, Swinburne had carried on an epistolary duel in the press. The epithets which the antagonists hurled at each other during their quarrel were both ingenious and indecorous, to say the least of it. When we returned to Swinburne we found that he had completed his study of Rowley; but he was evidently still in complete ignorance of the identity of the gentleman with whom he had been sharing the room. After we left the private library and were in a quiet corner, Walter said to Swinburne, " I say, do you know who it was you had sitting next you?" " No. Who was it? " asked the other. " Your *friend*, Furnivall," was my husband's illuminating reply. " *Tiens!* Was *that* the dog?" exclaimed Swinburne, without a trace of ill-humour.

During our Museum visit Mr. Fortescue took us into the King's Library and led us to a glass-case in which was enshrined the extremely rare first edition of " Hamlet." He unlocked the case, took out the precious volume, and, with great solemnity, placed it in Swinburne's hands. I shall never forget the look of rapturous awe on the poet's face as he turned the pages of the priceless book. He spoke no word. His wonder and reverence were too deep even for the customary "Ah-h-h! " He simply gazed—silent and transfixed. Then with a look of thanks in which I could see a trace of emotion, and with the inevitable bow he handed back the treasure to Mr. Fortescue. That gentleman did not immediately return the book to its place. With polite indulgence he handed it to me in order that I too might inspect it, and that I might be able to say I had read some of Shakespeare's " Hamlet " in a first edition.

To Swinburne and Walter it had been a most satisfactory day. To me it was a very memorable one.

During our walk from the Museum to the Holborn Restaurant where we were to lunch, A. C. S. talked with eloquence and with some excitement of the Elizabethans. It seemed queer to have for our objective instead of a Mermaid Tavern (or even a Rose and Crown!) an ultra-modern place like the Holborn. I made a remark to this effect as we took our places at a little side-table. But by this time the poet had come back to earth and was gazing all round him at the marble walls and the gold-latticed ceiling.

Walter told him that the fine marble pillars had come from Baron Grant's architectural " folly " at Kensington. It was quite characteristic of Swinburne that his comment on this should take the form of a question : "And who, may I ask, is Baron Grant? " The band had more interest for him than the Baron, and although he could not hear the music of the fiddlers, he seemed absorbingly interested in the antics of the conductor, who, violin in hand, was swaying his body about in the most wonderful rhythmic gyrations to the strains of " The Blue Danube."

As I watched Swinburne, I could not help speculating as to what his thoughts must be. He had chambers for a long time in the neighbourhood of the Holborn. In those far-off days—so Walter had told me—a dancing saloon stood on part of the site now occupied by the restaurant. Had the Bard, I wondered, ever gone into the old Holborn

Casino on the site of which he now sat sober and sedate, enjoying his luncheon and drinking the pint of claret that on this occasion replaced the usual beer. I was doomed to continue wondering, for allusions to the old uses of the floor failed to draw him. His expression became like that of the Heathen Chinee, " child-like and bland " To him the past was past indeed. The hectic roysterer of the sixties was gone : the grave and affable patrician of the twentieth century had taken his place.

After luncheon that ghastly contrivance known as a " four-wheeler " with the usual Rosinante between its shafts, was hailed for us, and we drove back to Putney.

In the cab Swinburne kept up an animated conversation about objects which he noticed *en route*. He was like a schoolboy out for a half-holiday.

At Piccadilly Circus we were " held up " for a bit. He put his head out of the window. "Ah! That's Swan and Edgar's. I *had* to go there with my mother when I was a little chap. She quite liked the place. I hated it. Fortnum and Mason's further down was more my sort of shop. It is associated in my mind with all sorts of good things to eat—delicious preserved fruit, *pâté de foie gras*, and everything else that is nice."

MISCELLANEA

During the journey home the friends discussed, *not* poetry, but the great question regarding the manufacture of this appetising dish. Walter told us horrid details about the sufferings of the wretched goose, confined and overfed with fattening foods until his liver should become just right for a perfect *pâté*. Swinburne gave a very quaint twist to the discussion at this point. Turning to Walter he said, " It always has been a puzzle to me why they send across the Channel for goose's liver when we have so many fat geese here." My husband looked at him with an obvious note of interrogation in his eyes. Swinburne smiled his ineffable smile and answered the unspoken question. " Fat geese in England!" he chirruped gleefully, " Well, there's —— and there's —— and there's ——." And he went on with a list of names of men eminent in literature, men whom I had been taught to regard with respect. We both laughed, so he proceeded : " Now *their* livers carefully treated ought to make excellent *pâté de foie gras*!"

I fear it may come as a shock to the aesthetic devotees of Swinburne to learn that the hideous word " bloke " was not foreign to his vocabulary. Coming from him it sounded dreadful, and when first I heard him use it, I was almost scandalised. I spoke to Walter about it, and he informed me that Swinburne had picked up this bit of slang from Dante Gabriel. The poet-painter maliciously revelled in the use of the *argot* of the slums as he had been told that the outside world believed that he and his friends always spoke in a " mediæval " style. My ear soon became inured to the prosaic monosyllable, for Swinburne would often say of a man he liked, "A very affable bloke, so-and-so." Such turns of speech would be out of place in a " Hymn to Proserpine "; but heard in the home circle they sounded—thanks to the speaker and his tone—quite pleasant when I got used to them.

The Bard made many quaint " finds " in the book line. One day he brought home from Wimbledon, " for a lark," as he expressed it, a tiny Coleridge in the Miniature Series. It contained " Kubla Khan " and other masterpieces, and was charmingly bound in brown suède. He was greatly excited and delighted that it included " Christabel,"—my husband's favourite among Coleridge's poems. He presented this little book as a veritable gem from Aladdin's Cave, saying not a word then about the magnificent " Christabel," illustrated by a facsimile of Coleridge's MS., which came to Walter a few days later.

Another " find " was a diminutive volume (two inches tall and a little less in width) entitled, *Verbum Sempiternum* or " The Thumb Bible." The work is a reprint by Longman (1849) of an opuscule by John Taylor the " water-poet," from an edition published in 1693, about forty years after that " literary bargee's " death. Taylor's art of summary produces something to make historians and prophets turn in their graves.

Swinburne's favourite passage in the little book was the address to " The Reader " It was a rare treat to hear him read the lines in his funny solemn tones and with appropriate gestures. I wish I could reproduce the accent and the movements. Here, however, are the verses :

> With care and pains out of the Sacred Book,
> This little Abstract I, for thee, have took.
> And with great reverence have I cull'd from thence,
> All things that are of Greatest consequence.
> And all I beg, when thou tak'st it in hand,
> Before thou judge, be sure to understand :
> And as thy kindness thou extend'st to me,
> At any time I'll do as much for thee.

THE HOME LIFE OF SWINBURNE

J. Taylor's method of conveying the truths of Scripture in tabloid form will be most easily appreciated by one example   The whole of the Book of Proverbs is disposed of in one couplet :

> The wisest Man that ever Man begot,
> In heav'nly Proverbs shews what's good, what's not.

However much " kindness " one " extends " to J. Taylor, it is difficult to believe that his " Thumb Bible " put much strain on his piety.

Swinburne's recitation of Taylor's introductory verses was invariably followed by a torrent of complimentary extravagance : " Prodigious and wonderful ! " " The greatest of us all."

I recall an incident which illustrates at once the casual manner in which Swinburne read ordinary correspondence and the attitude he adopted towards poets who had not yet " arrived."

On a date between 1897 and 1903, Countess Benckendorff sent to Swinburne for his perusal and advice a four-act play by Mr. Maurice Baring. A. C. S. wrote a reply, placed it with the play, and then forgot all about the matter. After his death the play and the letter were discovered. The following is the Bard's reply. It will be read with some surprise by his admirers :

MISCELLANEA

The Pines [undated].

MADAME,

Vous me demandez si votre nièce a du talent, et si elle peut espérer du succès.

Quant à cela, moi, qui vis hors du monde des lettres, je n'oserais pas hasarder un avis.

A. C. SWINBURNE.

Two things will appear strange to the reader in this communication. The first is how in the world Swinburne could have spoken of Mr. Baring as the niece of the Countess. Eventually a solution of the mystery flashed upon me. The poet evidently misread the word " Maurice " in the Countess's handwritten letter as " *ma nièce*." The whole blunder is characteristic. Mr. Maurice Baring, who, since the date of this little misunderstanding, has taken a recognised place among the literati of the day, will no doubt, be merely amused by it. I confess that I cannot explain Swinburne's description of himself as one living outside the world of letters. He who was honoured by its high priests, a voluminous contributor to the literature, poetical and critical, of his time—" outside the world of letters "! Why, he just palpitated with the life of that world. He knew no other, cared for no other. As to fearing "to hazard an opinion,"

235

he had no such fear when he took pen in hand nor did he seem restrained by any such feeling when he aired his opinions for the benefit of the home-circle. It was a case—this plea of severance from the world of letters—of " any excuse is better than none." He simply refused to look at the un-published work of any literary beginner, and there was no one in the world of letters to whom a novice could appeal with less hope of success than the author of "Atalanta in Calydon." It sounds a very unsympathetic attitude, but his day was too occupied by his own work for him to find any reserve of time to devote to the task of advising literary aspirants.

It seems hardly credible, but Swinburne one day gave me a sermon—a veritable sermon preached by a real priest of the Established Church. He had kept the thing by him for years, why, I cannot say. It was part of a collection of miscellaneous odds and ends that he had accumulated.

The author of the sermon was a certain Mr. Purchas who had a cure of souls in Brighton. Purchas had indulged in certain practices at the altar which had caused him to be "persecuted " by the evangelical party. The persecution caused the name of Purchas to be known far and wide—though his ritualistic candles and genuflexions were as trifles to the practices that are accepted now as a matter of course in thousands of our churches.

Now the Purchas persecution synchronised with the persecution, by the same party, of the author of the "Poems and Ballads." When Swinburne presented me with the printed discourse he expressed a hope that it would help to build me up in my most holy faith, and he told me that it had been accompanied by a letter in which the Brighton vicar expressed sympathy with the poet under the attacks which had been made upon him.

"I have never read the sermon," said A. C. S. to me, "and I am confident that my reverend correspondent never read the 'Poems and Ballads.' Had he glanced through them he would scarcely have ranked me in his holy regard as a sort of Christian martyr." He struck an attitude, finger-tips of both hands touching and held over his breast; his head bent sideways over one shoulder, and the whites of his eyes showing. One almost saw the halo which he imagined. A droll picture!

THE HOME LIFE OF SWINBURNE

We always tried to make Swinburne's birthday a festive occasion. On every anniversary shoals of congratulatory letters and telegrams and flowers would arrive at the house from strangers, at none of which would the poet give even a glance. But he would beam all over with pleasure at being remembered by his friends and relatives. It was a matter of some difficulty to select a suitable present for him other than a book. He never smoked and hated the very smell of tobacco. Walter told me that the Bard really liked sweet biscuits, and I was wont on anniversary occasions to present him with these dainties in a pretty box. Once to my great delight I came across a tin case designed to represent a series of volumes of Sir Walter Scott or Charles Dickens—it is so long ago that I forget which of the authors had been honoured in this way by the biscuit manufacturer. Nor does it matter very much—as the sequel will show. To all appearances it looked like a row of books in handsome bindings, and no one would have suspected that it was filled with a choice variety of toothsome cakes. In my unwisdom, I thought this would be quite *the* thing for his birthday present and prove a tremendous surprise. I purchased it imagining the while how pleased Swinburne would be. How he would inspect the supposed volumes! How he would try to pull one out, and his sensations when he discovered that a practical joke had been played on him and that he had been presented not with food for the mind, but with edible delectabilities! Fortunately, I told my husband of my purchase. Walter was aghast. When he saw the dummy books, he exclaimed with genuine horror, " Take it back at once. Get anything but that. Algernon would be so disgusted—so enraged to think that the mind of man could sink so low and insult literature to such a degree as to imitate the outside covers of his beloved authors in tin! And worse—far worse—the inside to be filled with biscuits! "

I took the offensive box back. And I purchased for the illustrious man the inevitable book.

CHAPTER XIX

THE TWO SWINBURNES

AFTER I had known Swinburne for some time—
say a year after my marriage—I became impressed with the fact that he possessed a dual
personality.

One Swinburne, and this the more lovable, was
the man we knew in the intimacy of the domestic
circle. The other was that aspect of himself which
was presented to the visitor, the acquaintance, or
the stranger within our gates.

When Walter and I were alone with the poet
he was absolutely natural, cheerful, sometimes full
of fun, and always interested in the little things
of life. When visitors were present, Swinburne
was quite a different man. He was restrained
and reticent until something was said about a
writer or an orator or an emperor whom at the
moment he either loved or loathed. Then the

sluices were opened. He burst into a flow of eulogy or vituperation, amazing and torrential.

If the presence of visitors brought out a Swinburne quite different from the gay and blithesome boy whom Walter and I knew, it also discovered a Swinburne physically different. Quite a number of those who were admitted to The Pines have, after departure, considered it quite the right thing to publish their recollections of the visit. And those persons have invariably noted the poet's deafness. Less excusable and sometimes, to speak bluntly, more detestable have been the physical personalia which have spiced articles on Swinburne in scores of magazines and newspapers.

Now what is the truth? As to the deafness, neither Walter nor I found the slightest difficulty in making him hear all we said, and that without unduly raising the voice. The same may be said of Mrs. Mason, Walter's sister, who was a great favourite of the poet and possessed a particularly soft and flexible voice. When Swinburne had become accustomed to the timbre of a voice as in the case of the individuals I have mentioned, conversation was perfectly easy as well as delightful. For Swinburne had a fine sense of humour; his persiflage was invariably brilliant, and his more serious utterances attained real eloquence. If visitors found him very deaf, I offer this explanation. He himself was conscious of defective hearing. He had the super-sensitiveness that is inseparable from the poetic temperament. The consciousness of his affliction reacted on his nerves, and his nerves, in their turn, reacted on his ear. He *was* hard of hearing, but in the presence of strangers his deafness temporarily increased.

As to certain spasmodic movements of Swinburne, a jerkiness of arms and shoulders, an uncontrollable mobility of legs and feet, I can only say that these signs of electrical overcharge, or defect in whatever Nature employs to maintain equilibrium, have been exaggerated by journalists beyond the limit of decency.

It is true that he was so carried away by excitement that he seemed unable to keep his feet or legs still when he recited either tragic or purely humorous sentences. In fact his whole body vibrated on these occasions.

But under ordinary circumstances—when strangers were not present—this eccentricity of sensitiveness was never observable. He made no convulsive movement in the intimacy of our domestic circle or when he was in the company of his relatives or old and much-loved friends.

THE TWO SWINBURNES

People with whom he was on less familiar terms sometimes affected him adversely with the result that inconsiderate or malicious writers have depicted Swinburne as a grotesquely restless being —a sort of human aspen.

My own opinion is that he was morbidly excited by the presence of those with whom he intuitively felt that he was not *en rapport*. To mental atmosphere he was wonderfully sensitive. The strangers who took note of his spasmodic movements—and seemed incapable of noting anything else—were blissfully unconscious of the fact that they themselves were the cause of the " symptom " which they deplored.

Swinburne was apt to resent the presence of persons with whom he knew himself to be entirely out of sympathy ; and he sometimes avenged himself by making with apparent seriousness, weird statements which were by no means his real convictions. Thus he has been debited with the assertion that he took no interest in the work of any poet who began to sing after the year 1850. This, to my knowledge, is untrue. He was deeply interested in such of the younger poets as evinced genius and wrote with distinction. For instance, of the poems of Mr. Alfred Noyes he spoke with genuine enthusiasm. He followed that writer's poetic career with pleasure and the appreciation of a critical poet for a fellow craftsman. He also had a great appreciation for the poetry of Dora Sigerson. Hence if he expressed to a visitor the opinion that in contemporary verse there was nothing new that was good and nothing good that was new, I feel justified in making the inference that Swinburne had been amusing himself by pulling that visitor's leg.

It is pleasant to recall the fact that the tribute which Mr. Noyes paid to the older poet on Swinburne's seventieth birthday was more fortunate than many a well-woven wreath. The ode to which I refer, and which immensely pleased Swinburne, contains these memorable lines:

> He needs no crown of ours, whose golden heart
> Poured out its wealth so freely in pure praise
> Of others: him the imperishable bays
> Crown, and on Sunium's height he sits apart,
> He hears immortal greetings this great morn!
> Fain would we bring, we also, all we may—
> Some wayside flower of transitory bloom,
> Frail tribute only born
> To greet the gladness of this April day,
> Then waste on Death's dark wind its faint perfume.

THE TWO SWINBURNES

In acknowledging the ode Swinburne wrote the following very charming letter:

The Pines,
March 29/7.

DEAR MR. NOYES,

Thank you very cordially for your fine verses, which have given me sincere pleasure.

I wish I could hope that my appreciation of your praise could give you half the pleasure that Hugo's too generous appreciation of my tributes repeatedly gave me.

Very truly yours,
A. C. SWINBURNE.

CHAPTER XX

THE PASSING OF THE POET

DURING my joyous married life, a dark shadow would occasionally obtrude itself on my sunlit path, but not long enough to cause me to feel more than a passing uneasiness. In the vague silhouette was scarcely discernible the menacing figure of Death, for as yet I knew nothing of the touch of his icy fingers. But if the Bard were ailing, or Walter himself out of sorts, a nameless " something " would creep into my heart. Then would Walter very simply and beautifully try to make me recognise in Death a kindly Harvester who one day might enter our home and take either himself or Swinburne to " that Kingdom beyond Orion " as he termed the peaceful abode of discarnate souls. He hated, however, to see the look of distress on my face that such talks produced. And when all cause for uneasiness had passed

246

away, he would always be the first to assure me that "All's right with the world." His compassionate heart was troubled by the thought inexpressibly painful to him, that if he were called away before Swinburne, there would be another besides myself—equally dear though in a different way—left to face life without his protecting, brotherly love.

Swinburne knew it too, and oh, how miserable he would be if Walter were at all ill. At such times, try as I might, I found it well-nigh impossible to imagine his life without Walter.

As the welfare of Algernon was always Walter's first consideration, he brooded deeply over this possible contingency, and deemed it advisable, in view of its arising, to make me acquainted with his inmost thoughts and desires regarding the care of his beloved friend. That Swinburne was spared the pain of losing his " best friend " (as he termed Walter in the dedication of " Tristram ") is an argument in favour of the existence of a Special Providence, or of that *Natura Benigna* of whom the author of " The Coming of Love " so beautifully sang.

I have already shown the reader how youthful

THE HOME LIFE OF SWINBURNE

Swinburne essentially was, and how the abounding energy of childhood seemed to radiate from him. Truly he, had the effect of belonging to no age in particular, although according to the calendar his years numbered sixty. He was so young in spirit, that meeting him so constantly, he seemed in my eyes a veritable Peter Pan, a simile which aptly pairs with Tennyson's description of him as "a reed through which all things blow into music."

He fostered the illusion that he was a child in more ways than one, and I unconsciously came to regard him, chiefly because of his heedlessness and utter carelessness of himself, as "the boy who wouldn't grow up."

So good was his general health, thanks no doubt to his regular habits, that he seemed immune from all the ills that flesh is heir to. Whenever I asked Walter after the health of the Bard, I was so accustomed to hearing my enquiry met with the cheery rejoinder, "Algernon is in great force," that it came as a shock to me in November, 1903, to learn that he was stricken by pneumonia. During Swinburne's illness, I received daily bulletins from Walter reporting the condition of his friend. I remember vividly the anxiety I felt on first seeing in the street the orange placard of the *Pall Mall Gazette* announcing in big black letters " Serious Illness of Mr. Swinburne."

I had never known him to be dangerously ill before, and although his state until the crisis had passed seriously alarmed the household at The Pines, he himself, when out of danger, refused to believe he had been as ill as he undoubtedly had been. He made the worst possible patient in the world, and hated the sight of the nurses to whose care, much to his own annoyance, his life was entrusted. *He* didn't see the necessity for nurses, and resented their installation in no very polite language. When I saw him after his recovery, and, with the understanding of one who had lain at death's door with pneumonia two years before, congratulated him on what was considered his narrow escape, he pooh-poohed all mention of the " disagreeable time," as he called it, through which he had passed, and only chafed because he felt temporarily weak.

His waywardness at this time made poor Walter chronically anxious about him, and I would hear a variety of reports, more or less amusing, of the Bard's irresponsibility and imprudent indifference to the rules laid down for a convalescent. A fear of a relapse never entered *his* head, although, needless to say, it was the dread of everybody else.

THE HOME LIFE OF SWINBURNE

He recovered so marvellously that, so far as out-
ward appearances went, he was soon as well as
ever. But Walter feared the effects of an illness
that is apt to leave a trace behind it in some
form or another. In the case of Swinburne it
left, apparently without his knowing it, a chest-
weakness which rendered him slightly more
susceptible to cold. He never complained, but
Walter became very worried if he came home
at all wet from a shower. No excuses about not
needing to change or keeping luncheon waiting
were of the least use. Walter fidgeted until
he had put on dry things, and refused to look
happy until he saw the Bard appear, high and dry
and jubilant, to take his place at the table.

Being thus guarded from his own disdain of
danger from cold, Swinburne's life went tranquilly
on with never an ache or pain. But he was
vulnerable after all, and when in 1909 the first
chilliness of Spring brought with it a visitation of
influenza, he was one of its victims.

The last episode of his life was preceded by an
attack towards the end of March on Walter by the
same malady. My mother had succumbed to it
only three weeks before, and my alarm can be
better imagined than described. The doctor,
however, did not take a serious view of Walter's

condition, though he ordered him to go to bed at once. Now, Walter, even more than Swinburne, disliked staying in bed, however out of sorts he felt, so he did not obey the doctor's order, but tried to keep up the whole of the day, contending that it depressed him horribly to stay in bed when he wanted to be up. The next day his temperature had risen, and willy-nilly he could not get up.

Luckily I was in very good health, and was appointed to be my husband's nurse Walter's chief concern now, in spite of feeling exceedingly ill, was how to deal with Algernon—how to account for his non-appearance at the mid-day meal, and how to keep him out of his sick room. The fear of his contracting the malady if he stayed by his friend's bedside, and the danger of a fresh attack of pneumonia, filled our minds with nervous apprehension on the Bard's behalf. To alarm Swinburne unnecessarily was a thing to guard against, and Walter's non-appearance at luncheon would be certain to give rise to comment. Duly coached by Walter how to meet questions, I was deputed to say that as he had a " slight cold " he was taking his meals in his room for that day.

The first thing that met Swinburne's eye when

he came to lunch was Walter's empty place opposite him. After a minute or two he turned to me with the question I could see before I heard it, " Where's Walter? " I repeated what I had been authorised to say.

" Oh ! " exclaimed Algernon, looking surprised and disappointed, but not otherwise perturbed, " I'll go and see how he is after luncheon."

Before taking his usual siesta he presented himself in Walter's bedroom. He expressed his solicitude, and commiserated him upon being forced to keep to his room. " But," added he, quite cheerfully, and with never a trace of any misgiving, " I can just as well read to you here, so you'll see me at the usual time ready to go on with our book." He looked towards us with a happy smile on his face as he made this announcement, and with the prospect of being able to indulge in one of his few little pleasures he went to his own bedroom. The book he referred to was " Ivanhoe," and for weeks past, with unfailing regularity, upon awakening refreshed from his afternoon sleep, he had gone into Walter's study to read for an hour or so from the pages of this beautiful romance.

Punctually at the appointed hour, a tap was heard at the bedroom door, and there stood the

Bard patiently awaiting permission to enter. He walked straight up to Walter's bedside and took a seat beside him. He had " Ivanhoe " in his hand all ready to· begin. Before reading, he gave a brief synopsis of the events occurring in the preceding chapter, and of those about to follow—a usual custom with him when reading a book they both knew well. Then, looking at me for an instant, expecting me either to get up and leave them alone, or sit where I was and listen, he turned to the place where they had left off the day before and asked " Shall we begin? " But Walter suggested that he might catch his cold if he sat near him for even half-an-hour, and suggested that they should postpone the reading till to-morrow, when they would be able to continue as usual. Swinburne looked woefully disappointed at being thus banished, and turning his gaze in my direction, he enquired, "And will Clara stay and read it to you then?" Walter assured him I would do nothing of the kind, and promised that only he should continue the narrative, explaining that as he was *really not at all well*, the doctor thought it advisable that I should be at hand to wait on him.

Swinburne appeared satisfied with this answer, and expressed his sorrow at his friend's condition.

He seemed depressed, and just before leaving the room he said to me with rather a pathetic ring in his voice, and more than a suspicion of a sigh, "Ah, you are the privileged one!" But with the anticipation of resuming "Ivanhoe" on the morrow, he regained his equanimity. Later, when he returned with the evening paper, in which he had discovered some item of news that he felt compelled to impart to us, he was as jolly as ever, and was allowed to stay for a little while and read it out.

The next day was cold and blustering, and Walter could guess what the weather would be like outside. He sent me to ascertain if Swinburne had gone out, and if he was still indoors, I was told to ask him not to go for his usual four-mile tramp across the Common. But he had already started— a little earlier than usual—a circumstance which I explained as an attempt to obtain a remedy for a surfeit of his own society.

All the time he was out, Walter was wondering about him and fuming over his recklessness, for of course we knew he had not put on an over-coat despite the keenness of the air and the lowering clouds.

As soon as we heard him mounting the stairs—it was easy to hear him, for he had a habit of noisily kicking each stair in his ascent—the " Colonel "* went out to the landing to meet him and tell him to make haste and change.

He appeared in the doorway, boisterously happy, but very wet. He had enjoyed the exercise because of the rain, not in spite of it, and looked exhilarated and well. Walter remonstrated with him for venturing out on such a day, telling him that such weather was enough to chill anybody to death. Of course the Bard could not agree with him. He always contended rain never did *him* any harm, and that he liked to feel it beating against his face.

What a " Peter Pan " he looked as he stood there laughing, and not in the least concerned about himself! But he *had* caught cold, and when in the late afternoon he paid us another visit, " to see how Walter was getting on," he looked weary and listless, in strange contrast to the picture he had presented in the earlier part of the day. He did not even suggest another chapter or two of " Ivanhoe," which he had so earnestly desired the afternoon before, and went downstairs looking as unlike himself as possible.

On April 2nd, in order to prevent a repetition of

* My husband's secretary, Edmund Hake, called " Colonel " as a joke.

his escapade of the day before, the weather still
continuing cold and damp, some little time before
the hour for him to start, Walter sent a very
peremptory message to him absolutely forbidding
him to go out. The next morning we were considerably surprised to learn that he had not left
his room, and had requested the maid to bring
his breakfast up to him, as he intended to stay
where he was. She told us that he seemed quite
bright, and was laughing over the book he was
reading as he lay in bed. Such an unusual
proceeding naturally alarmed us, for Swinburne
despised the *malade imaginaire*. Walter looked
very worried, and I remember how amused he was
at my knowledge of the Bard's funny little ways
when I endeavoured to cheer him by suggesting
that perhaps he was only bored, and was staying
in bed because he (Walter) was doing likewise.
When the doctor arrived to pay his daily visit,
my husband asked him to " go in and have a look
at Swinburne."

The friends' bedrooms adjoined, and the doors
being left open it was quite easy to hear all that
the doctor said. Owing to Swinburne's deafness,
he had to speak with his voice considerably raised
in order that Algernon could catch his words. I
remember vividly hearing him ask in a loud and

cheery tone, "And how are you, sir?" I could not catch the poor Bard's reply. I expect he was none too pleased to receive a visit from one of the faculty. Presently the voice of the doctor was again heard telling A. C. S. how much more comfortable he would be in his big study downstairs, where there he would be in his big study downstairs, where there was only a gas stove. We anxiously awaited the doctor's verdict, and in a few minutes he appeared announcing that Swinburne was very ill, and that he feared complications as the illness developed.

Two trained nurses were quickly on the scene, and Sir Thomas Barlow was telephoned for to consult with Dr. White. But Sir Thomas Barlow was away spending Easter on the Continent, and Sir Douglas Powell was called in. Both doctors took a grave view of the case, and when I next saw Swinburne he was lying on the little bed that had been hastily prepared for him in his library. Even then he was occasionally delirious, and our anxiety deepened. A nurse was stationed on the landing outside his room with the door open, for in his lucid moments it would have irritated him to see a strange woman sitting by his bedside. Walter prepared both nurses for the possibility that their presence might excite their distinguished patient to the utterance of

" Elizabethan language," and requested them not to go near him except when absolutely necessary. Upstairs in his room, although by now he was gaining strength, Walter lay in bed strained and nervous, wondering what the issue would be. At intervals I would go down to Swinburne to take little messages to him from Walter. I found that he absolutely refused to allow the nurse to administer oxygen. Though he was sometimes delirious, he was conscious enough to know that a stranger was bending over him, and when she attempted to place the tube near his mouth he beat it away with his hands, crying out in an enfeebled voice, " Take it away, take it away ! "

But the nurse's science told her that oxygen was necessary, and accordingly Walter's influence was asked for and promptly used. Acting as Walter's proxy, I went to Swinburne's bedside and told him that Walter considered the oxygen to be akin to a sea-breeze, and that it would do him all the good in the world. He opened his eyes and gladly allowed me to put the tube quite near his mouth as he inhaled the vapour without another murmur.

It was painful sometimes to watch him hurl the blankets off his chest and shoulders as he tossed about in a state of high fever. No sooner had the nurse or I replaced them than he would again try to fling them off   Occasionally he would talk wildly for a long while without stopping. I remember the nurse asked me in what language he was talking. I could catch a word here and there as he muttered long sentences with astonishing rapidity, and an occasional phrase in his disjointed monologue made me guess that he was speaking or reciting in Greek. I told Walter about this: he did not contradict me, pathetically sighing, "Ah, poor boy, poor boy!"

I have no wish to start an occult legend, yet I feel my account of Swinburne's death would be incomplete if I did not mention a curious sense of hearing presaging chords of music which invaded me whenever I entered his room and found him either breathing heavily or moaning in broken accents in uneasy sleep. All was so still and quiet in that book-lined chamber, and save for his low murmurs, not a sound, even from without, could be heard.

It did not matter now which of us held the oxygen to his parched and feverish lips, for he knew no one.

The doctor called again towards evening and gave no ray of hope. He knew Swinburne must die. Double pneumonia was fast gaining mastery over him in rapid strides. Many letters and telegrams of congratulation on his birthday

(April 5th) still lay unopened on his table, and the lovely bunch of daffodils that a lady, a stranger, had brought were still fresh and blooming. At any other time how both he and Walter would have rhapsodised over these flowers that told of the arrival of Spring. I know Shakespeare's lovely lines from " The Winter's Tale " would assuredly have been quoted. They were so intensely admired by both, and not only at this season, but often at other times would I hear of the

Daffodils
That come before the swallow dares, and take
The winds of March with beauty.

Soon after Dr. White had left the room, the nurse turned to me and asked Swinburne's age. I told her he had just passed his seventy-third birthday. She made no comment, but ejaculated with a gloomy significance of tone which I think I shall never forget, " Ah, Ah! " It was *this* tone, far more than the doctor's foreboding expression as he cast his eyes towards poor unconscious Algernon, that impressed me with a feeling of doom.

Late that same evening when I was sitting beside Walter, I told him how unhappy I had felt all day, and how the nurse's exclamation had

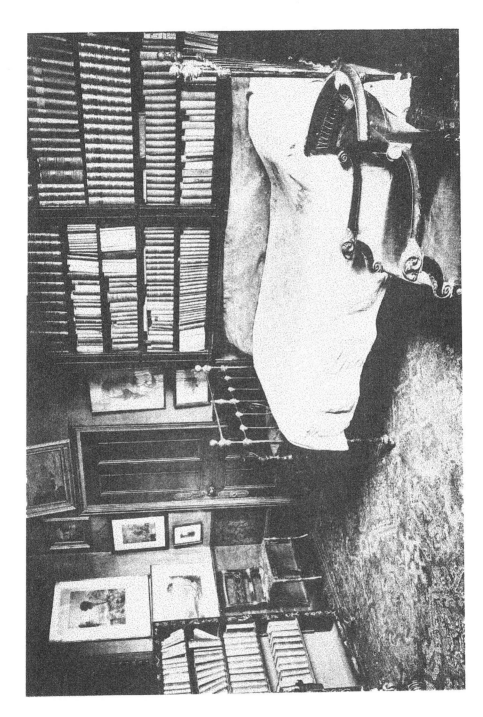

affected me. It was then about ten o'clock, and we heard the night-nurse pass the door on her way downstairs.

After thinking deeply for some time, as if he, too, felt the end was approaching, Walter turned to me and said, " Clara, help me on with my dressing-gown. I'm going down to see Algernon." He was very weak, and when I helped him into the coat as he stood on the floor for the first time in ten days he trembled. With my aid he got to the top of the stairs, and holding on to the banisters succeeded in descending the staircase. As I watched his progress from the landing and saw him enter Swinburne's room, I felt my heart beating violently, and for a moment I seemed to stop breathing.

He was not gone very long, and when he returned to the bedroom it was some time before he could speak. Then it was only to strain me to him and murmur in a broken voice, " Oh, Clara, Clara! " I knew just how he must be feeling, and for some time neither of us spoke. I sat holding his hand and pressing it gently. After a few minutes he returned my pressure, looked up bravely in my face, and with never a break in his voice said, " Go and tell the night-nurse to come here and speak to me." When she appeared he told her in a quiet collected tone, "If you see any change in the night, come and tell me." But there was no occasion to arouse him, and it was not till about ten o'clock the next morning (April 10) that Swinburne passed very quietly and peacefully away. He had been ill just a week.

What the death of Algernon meant to Walter cannot be expressed in words. I don't think he ever got over it.

But weak and shaken as he was, his faculties had to be on the alert, and he at once braced himself to the business ahead of him in connection with Swinburne's funeral. There was much that necessitated his immediate attention, and for the time being he was obliged to devote himself to it.

In the afternoon of April 10 we received a visit from his and Algernon's old friend, William M. Rossetti, who came down to Putney accompanied by his daughter Helen directly he received the tragic news.

The sight of this dear and devoted comrade at such a moment affected my poor Walter to tears, and when I returned to the room after leaving them for some time, I found William's arm round his shoulders as he endeavoured to comfort him. But what particularly arrested my eye at that moment was the photograph that lay on the bed; it had not been there before, and they had evidently been discussing it. It was one of D. G. Rossetti's drawings, " The Question," which represents a young man in the prime of life gazing resolutely into the impenetrable face of the Sphinx, who is represented as a creature half-woman and half-beast, with outstretched wings on the shoulders. A youth on the threshold of manhood has fallen on his knees by the wayside, bent on solving the great riddle, whilst an old man, leaning on his staff, is advancing from the right with feeble gait to ask of the Sphinx the great question, " Whither? "

This incident made a deep impression on my mind, for though I did not know what the conversation had been, it was clear it had to do with thoughts suggested by the passing of Algernon.

How splendid and noble Swinburne looked as he lay dead in that room where for more than thirty years he had worked and thought. There was the same calm and placid look of well-being that had characterised him in life. I was so struck by the likeness he bore to Tennyson, of whom a beautiful photogravure portrait after the painting by Millais was hanging in the next room, that I called Dr. White in to look at it. Each man possessed a magnificent domed forehead; Tennyson's head rose higher above the frontal bones, but the breadth *across* the head which was so noticeable a feature in Swinburne when alive, appeared less so in death and heightened the resemblance.

When I took William Rossetti into the death-chamber he was very deeply affected as he gazed for the last time upon the features of his friend. And he, who had known Swinburne for so many years, agreed with me when I pointed out the resemblance to Tennyson.

After William and his daughter had gone, I went alone into the familiar room, and gazed my ll into Swinburne's face, and thought and thought for a long while. In the stillness, I felt a sense of cal i steal over me. Then, perhaps because I had seen the book he had been reading before he was brought downstairs ("Investigations of the Chevalier Dupin") my thoughts drifted to Poe's Raven, whose "Nevermore" was sounding in my brain. And as I thought of the bereaved hero of that poem and of the mystic bird perched eternally above his door, I involuntarily looked at the portrait of Mazzini, hanging above the bureau in the chamber of death. That melancholy face of fixed resolve seemed that of a Raven transformed to a human being, and I almost imagined I heard the " Nevermore."

And then I felt I wanted to see Swinburne's eyes once again, even though it were in death. I ventured to raise his eyelids very gently, and found that they looked just as I had so often seen them, infinitely kind. With the memory of all he meant to me I left the room.

CHAPTER XXI

TELEGRAMS and letters from all quarters arrived by every post. Walter was far too ill to answer them ; but to special friends of his and Swinburne's he commissioned me to reply by telegram. I remember an especially long one, I sent to the dead poet's friend, Lady Ritchie.

It was a very trying time, relieved by visits from near and dear friends. Mr. and Mrs. Holman Hunt arrived one day, and offered the rare balm of understanding sympathy that goes direct to the heart. Mr. Ernest Rhys, the Welsh poet, and Mr. James Douglas, a frequent visitor and special friend of both my husband and Swinburne, came on alternate afternoons, and did Walter much good. Dear Lady Archibald Campbell assured us with characteristic optimism that " Our dear Bard is just as happy as ever in yonder

Sphere." In beautiful and touching fashion, the
Ranee of Sarawak paid her last adieux to one
towards whom she felt a very tender regard.
Walter was not well enough to see her on the day
she called. She asked me, I well remember, in a
voice trembling with tears, to be allowed to go
into Swinburne's room and place quite near his
heart the posy of flowers she had brought. I felt
she would prefer to be alone in the death-chamber
and did not follow her. She stayed for a little
while to think her own sweet thoughts in solitude,
and when she reappeared she was deeply moved.
Afterwards, when we were in the drawing-room,
I heard again from her lips of the visits (often
alluded to by the Bard) which he had paid to her
son Bertram when he was ill and found difficulty
in recovering his health after a severe illness.
These visits had been a pleasure to the poet as well
as to the invalid, whom dear Swinburne had much
cheered. The memory of the poet's kindness
towards her suffering boy had sown the seeds of
deep and lasting gratitude in the Ranee's tender
heart. By this time the library where Swinburne
lay resembled a fairy bower, so full was it of beauti
ful flowers. Whilst scores of wreaths were ranged
round his bier, I placed on the coffin itself only a
tribute of laurel leaves " To Algernon with

Walter's love.'' When I told my husband what I had done, he said tenderly, '' That was right, dear.''

A sweet token that would, I know, have pleased the poet more than any other, was the little bunch of Spring flowers sent by a tiny admirer. Between ruled lines, on a card on which was easily discernible the pencil marks of the composer of the sentence, and inked over by an obviously *very* youthful hand, was this inscription :

'' From Robin ''
The little boy to whom Mr. Swinburne
used to wave his hand.

Lovely was the day that saw Swinburne's mortal remains taken to their last resting-place. Allowing that the sea would have been the ideal cemetery for the man who sang its glories more divinely than any other Englishman, no other place on earth could have been found more appropriate than the little Island he loved. As the writer of an Isle of Wight guide-book remarks, the churchyard at Bonchurch is so beautiful that, to quote Shelley, it might make one '' in love with death '' to think one would be buried in so sweet a place.

One incident which occurred on the journey across the Solent created an indelible impression on those who witnessed it.

We had reached the point where for a few minutes the little steamer was apparently out of sight of land. The sea was quite calm, and as I stood on the upper deck looking down at the tarpaulin-covered coffin in the bows of the deck below me, one great sunlit wave came sweeping towards us as if to enfold that dark burden in its embrace. Right over the bows and the coffin the white glory of the foam swept as if to take farewell of the sea's great lover in one last caress. This incident will remind lovers of Shelley of the legend of the sea-bird which hovered over his pyre.

That Swinburne's funeral was *not* the unorthodox ceremony he had desired was plain enough to all those who saw it. For myself, speaking as an eye-witness, the simple Church of England Service was very beautiful, and I do not believe that Swinburne in his heart of hearts was so violently agnostic and opposed to Christianity as his hatred of the crimes of bigotry has led people to think. His letters to his mother in the book by his cousin, Mrs. Leith, " The Boyhood of Algernon Charles Swinburne," show what sane and sweet ideas regarding the after-life he entertained. To her whom he loved so dearly he wrote in 1892 :—
" It is so beautiful and delightful to think of 'being

together when this life is over,' as you say, and of seeing things no longer ' in a glass darkly,' and all who have ever tried to do a little bit of what they thought right being brought together—if what they thought right was not absolutely wicked and shocking like the beliefs of persecutors, and understanding and loving each other—that I sometimes feel as if it ought hardly to be talked about."

Undoubtedly Swinburne did not deny the existence of a life beyond the grave.

Again I quote from Mrs. Leith's book in another letter to his mother written in 1885 just after the death of Victor Hugo: " When I think of his (Hugo's) intense earnestness of faith in a future life and a better world than this, and remember how fervently Mazzini always urged upon all who loved him the necessity of that belief and the certainty of its actual truth, I feel very deeply that they must have been right—or at least that they should have been—however deep and difficult the mystery which was so clear and transparent to their inspired and exalted minds may seem to such as mine.

I don't know what conclusions my husband and Algernon had come to in different conversations on the vexed subjects of immortality and funeral rites; but I understood that the poet expressed a wish that orthodox ritual should be omitted at his funeral. Unfortunately his will conveyed no instructions respecting the disposal of his remains; and though Walter did all he could to have the funeral conducted in harmony with the dead man's views, he was far too unwell to exert the necessary pressure or exercise the required ingenuity to have things done in accordance with them.

To Sir John Swinburne (the poet's cousin) who acompanied me down to Bonchurch, my husband gave as lucid instructions as was possible in telegrams regarding that part of the religious service which was to be performed; and the night before the ceremony, the Rector of Bonchurch had been advised that in deference to the poet's wishes the Church of England Burial Service must not be used. In the railway-carriage during the journey to Ventnor, Sir John rehearsed his part to me, to Swinburne's cousin, Lord Gwydyr, and to the latter's son-in-law, Sir John Henniker Heaton, until he quite tired us out.

We were all under the impression that everything would go as arranged, and that the service would be conducted with due regard for the wishes of the illustrious dead. But, in the circumstances, there was nothing to be done. The Rector of Bonchurch met the coffin as it left the hearse and immediately began reading the first lines of the Burial Service as the mourners walked in procession to the grave. There was no preliminary service held in the Church, but apart from this concession —possibly an important one—Swinburne's body was consigned to the grave in accordance with the rites of the Established Church of England.

As an old friend of the poet tersely remarked after the obsequies were over, "You see, you can't even get *buried* the way you want without your relations interfering."

The Free-Thinkers' press was very acrimonious after Swinburne's funeral. Pamphlets galore arrived for Walter, but I took care that he saw none of them. Also for me, for the writers imagined I was the person responsible for the funeral service, seeing I had represented my husband at the graveside. I was invited to enter into controversy with a variety of persons who deal in Free Thought. If they had searched the globe, they could not have fastened on anyone more unfitted to take part in such a duel of words, and the matter ended with my silence. When Walter died in June, 1914, and they again attacked him— or his memory—I appealed to my friend, Mr. Edward Clodd, at whose charming house at Aldeburgh I then stayed for a day or two, to put matters right. He replied to the offending journal thus :

In a too cursory reading of the paragraphs by " Mimnermus " in your July issue, his comment on the late Theodore Watts-Dunton's assumed permission of the use of the orthodox ritual at Swinburne's funeral escaped my notice.

Will you permit me to say that the assumption is wholly unwarranted? Not long before his death Mr. Watts-Dunton repeated to me his feeling of deep vexation, not only as to the mockery of recital of the orthodox ritual, but also as to the placing of a cross over the remains of a friend who was anti-Christian to the end. For such actions the relations of Algernon Swinburne, and they alone, are responsible.

EDWARD CLODD.

After Swinburne had been taken to his last resting-place, the house seemed strange. His room looked a desert, and everything there, particularly the pictures of ships, reminded one of those little things that had gone to make up his life. Especially was this the case with a charming little water-colour, by C. Jeffcock, of Southwold Beach, with " Boats in Brilliant Sunshine," which he had acquired but a short time before his death and was very fond of—and justly, for one could almost feel the wind blowing from the sea through the sails of the boats on shore.

THE HOME LIFE OF SWINBURNE

It was less sad to look at the portraits of his friends who had gone before him. There was Sir Edward Burne-Jones—"Ned," as Swinburne always called him—standing in an unstudied attitude on some tall steps in his studio, palette and brushes in hand, at work on one of his large canvases. A splendid photo of William Morris occupied a place "on the line" near the door. Walter Savage Landor also was placed conveniently for the worshipping eye. And his books, there they were, serried rows of them, just as Swinburne's dying eyes last saw them. Walter never went near the room for weeks . .

Of all the many photographs of Swinburne, none looked so much like the Algernon I knew as the last one he had taken. It looked so like him that when he died we had this almost life-size portrait of him placed over the mantel-piece in our sitting-room. We felt it brought him nearer to us as we sat there.

Quite soon after his death Walter and I were sitting together one evening after dinner when the postman brought what I thought was a letter for Walter. The contents moved him deeply, and I noticed the tears gathering in his eyes. Turning to me he said, "Read this, Clara; it's the loveliest thing I've ever read about dear Algernon." It was a poem by Alfred Noyes. I tried to read the lines to myself without a lump coming into my throat, but I failed in the attempt, and in turn my eyes, too, became so dim that I could hardly read the words. This is how the death of Swinburne affected one of our finest singers:

IN MEMORY OF SWINBURNE.
I.

April from shore to shore, from sea to sea,
   April in heaven and on the springing spray
   Buoyant with birds that sing to welcome May
And April in those eyes that mourn for thee;
" This is my singing month; my hawthorn tree
   Burgeons once more," we seemed to hear thee say,
   " This is my singing month; my fingers stray
Over the lute. What shall the music be?"

And April answered with too great a song
   For mortal lips to sing or hearts to hear,
Heard only of that high invisible throng
   For whom thy song makes April all the year!
" My singing month, what bringest thou?" Her breath
Swooned with all music, and she answered—" Death."

Some months later, when the Summer sun was shining brightly, Walter and I looked over a sparkling sea. The delight of reading out of doors was healing and restful, and although Walter was shattered in health, it was good to be alive and happy together. One morning he produced a book from his pocket, and laying it on my lap, he said, "This is Algernon's 'Ivanhoe': do you go on reading where he left off. We'll finish it as we sit here looking at the waves." There was a bookmark in Chapter XLI, so there was not much to read before the end. That lovely incident, the most thrilling in the story, the rescue of the beautiful Rebecca by Wilfred of Ivanhoe, is related in the final four chapters. I read them to Walter in a way I knew he would enjoy. But as I neared the end, his eyes looked wistfully sad, for his thoughts had flown, as had mine, to him who had preceded me in reading aloud from the book. Little had Walter anticipated when he told Algernon that I should not take his place, that his promise would be unfulfilled, and that even in this small matter of finishing "Ivanhoe" I should be, as in Walter's sick-room, "the privileged one."

As I closed the book, I pictured the quiet grave near the sea at Bonchurch as I had seen it on the day the dear Bard was laid to rest. Walter fell to talking in a dreamy, ruminating way of Algernon. "Dear boy, dear boy, what a splendid, lovable fellow he was! I miss him dreadfully." And he added to himself *sotto voce* · "There's nobody for me to talk poetry with now." It was impos-

sible for me or anybody to fill the blank in
Walter's life that the death of Algernon had made.
To take up the threads of life again after such a
tear in the web was not easy. He was even inclined
at this time to view life as a " Long Street of
Tombs," although he was naturally richly endowed
with gaiety.

I was desirous that he should regain health, and
gather as much strength as he could, and was
very properly opposed to the formation in him of
any sense of obligation to sit down and begin
writing Swinburne's " Life." The inconsiderate
people who expected him to devote his scanty
energy to biographical toil were not viewed by me
with sympathy or even patience. Neither friends
nor the public were intimately concerned with his
personal welfare; I was. I remember that one
day, when a visitor began descanting on the desirability of my husband's writing Algernon's
" Life," I cut short his eloquence by declaring,
with frowns and scowls, that biography was mere
stodge and Baedekerism, and that nobody wanted
any more of it. Walter was highly amused by
" Serjeant Clara Buzfuz," as he playfully called
me on this occasion. I knew my little prejudiced
opinion was worth absolutely nothing but, nevertheless, Walter was comforted by it and that was

all *I* cared about. I got so used to snubbing people who asked about the unwritten " Life " by Watts-Dunton that Walter, with his tongue in his cheek, would account for its absence by saying, " Clara knows if she would but speak." So if people wonder why Watts-Dunton wrote no "Life of Swinburne" let them in a measure blame me. Had I chosen I could at least have goaded him to the production of the " Life "; but my understanding love for him told me that his strength was not great enough to justify him in undertaking so emotional and tiring a task.

That Walter did wish to write such a book, I emphatically assert. He knew his subject from A to Z, but he never got further than writing a "Supplemental Note " to the eighteenth impression of the " Selections from Swinburne's Poems. He did this after the Christmas of 1913, and when I read his MS. a stab pierced my heart on reading the introductory lines and opening sentence of the little article :

> Time driveth onward fast,
> And in a little while our lips are dumb.

Let me take warning by these noble words of Tennyson : let me remember that I may never live to write my reminiscences of Swinburne, much as I desire to do so.

That literature is the poorer for not possessing
a sympathetic and complete " Life of Swinburne "
by Watts-Dunton, is undeniable, but it is not
likely that Swinburne would have welcomed any
such work by anyone. It was George Meredith
who declared, " I will horribly haunt the man who
writes my biography." Swinburne never went as
far as that. On the other hand, he never mentioned whom he had selected to write his Life, as
did Dante Gabriel Rossetti. But if Swinburne
had been obliged to choose a biographer, he would
certainly have selected Walter, the friend whom
he pronounced " the first critic of our time—
perhaps the largest-minded and surest-sighted of
any age."

It is a pretty well known fact that Rossetti
wished Theodore Watts more than anyone else
to write his Life. Walter used often to say to me
when he fell to talking of this wondrous and very
dear friend, " Gabriel told me everything," and
I know dear Swinburne told him everything too.
We all know that Walter could not stand far
enough away from Rossetti to write his life, and
that W. M. Rossetti, after waiting for years for
Walter to produce it, assumed the rôle of
biographer himself.

Tout passe, tout lasse, tout casse, says **the**

proverb, but the immortal works of Rossetti and Swinburne will always remain without needing assistance from " Lives."

It is not for me even to whisper of the place that Swinburne holds, and perhaps will ever hold, as the greatest lyrical poet of his century. Generations yet unborn will marvel at the white magic which his poetry exerts even upon comparatively commonplace people.

George Meredith, in the letter he wrote to Walter—the last he ever penned before he passed away about a month after the death of Swinburne—says : " Song was his natural voice. He was the greatest of our lyrical poets—of the world's, I could say, considering what a language he had to wield."

For me, it is with a satisfaction not to be measured in words that I regard the privilege vouchsafed me in being able to call that simple-minded great English gentleman, Algernon Charles Swinburne, my friend.

CHAPTER XXII

A POET'S GRAVE

BRILLIANT sunshine and genial warmth had transformed our British Autumn into a gorgeous St. Luke's Summer. On the Sunday in October, 1920, when I revisited Bonchurch to look at Swinburne's grave it was hard to believe that the words " Chill October " had ever been used by a famous painter to describe the tenth month. Summer blooms were absent and birds were silent; but the churchyard still looked like a beautiful garden.

The big crowd of people that filled it on the day of the poet's funeral naturally precluded the possibility of appreciating the beauties of the spot. Even had the crowd been smaller, my mournful feelings would have crushed any desire to take in the little landscape, and I was practically seeing it in its ensemble for the first time. As I approached the entrance gates, I could hear the notes of the church organ, for the service was going on.

Almost the first thing that attracts the visitor's attention on entering the churchyard is the group of graves in which members of the Swinburne family are buried. Enclosed behind an iron rail are five of these sepulchres. The stone slab above each is distinguished by a characteristic design, something between a cross and an anchor, very much in keeping with the ideas of a sailor, and chosen, no doubt, by Admiral Swinburne on that account. Of these five graves, those of Algernon and Isabel are side by side, for the eldest and the youngest of the Admiral's children were the last to go.

Beyond this group is a second one in which under the same kind of slabs, are the remains of the poet's Mother and Father, Lady Jane Swinburne, Admiral Swinburne, and his sister Edith, who was the first of the family to die. Personally—if I may obtrude my personal opinion—I found the plain stone that covers Swinburne's frail body satisfactory and suitable. As I looked at the simple inscription of name and date, I reflected that it was not the great poet that lay there; it was the son of a

patrician house.   It was good to think that he
who sang :

> I will go back to the great sweet Mother,
>   Mother and lover of men, the sea.
> I will go down to her, I and none other.
>   Close with her, kiss her, and mix her with me,

slept within sound of the music of the sea he loved
so well and so glorified in his verse, but what
" Swinburne " stands for lives in the hearts and
minds of the countless thousands who love the
outpourings of his spirit.

While I was meditating in this way, the service
in the church ended.   The little congregation
trooped out, and I found myself addressed by a
tall, handsome old man who identified me with the
lady whom he had seen at Algernon's funeral.   He
was accompanied by a much younger man, his son,
who informed me he also remembered me, having
seen me when he called on my husband at The
Pines.   But what particularly interested me was
the fact that all his life the elder man, a Mr. Daniel
Day, had had dealings with the Swinburne family,
being a sort of bailiff or agent for them.   He was
also a builder, decorator, undertaker, and I don't
know what else.   Moreover, he was one of the
churchwardens of the Parish Church.

THE HOME LIFE OF SWINBURNE

The affectionate respect with which he spoke of the poet's family, " all dead and gone now," touched me deeply. When he mentioned the name of Lady Jane he lowered his voice in reverence. I had heard from Walter's lips of the effect of her death on Algernon, and as this survivor reminded me of the poet's grief when she was buried, and we talked on, I could see how disturbed he was at the idea of Swinburne being thought an atheist. Mr. Day, I imagine, knew little, if anything at all, of the writings of A. C. S. This would perhaps account for his indignation over the charge of atheism sometimes levelled against the writer of the " Hymn to Man." He had an answer to that grave charge. He assured me that, after the conclusion of the burial service of Charlotte, Algernon knelt at the graveside with his sisters Alice and Isabel, and prayed. That Swinburne knelt, I can easily believe. His innate chivalry and his affection for his sisters would ensure the kneeling. But what, I wonder, was the nature of the prayer. " I know he was no atheist," reiterated Mr. Day, and when he tentatively touched on " things he wrote," I thought it kind to say that I believed Swinburne's agnosticism to be much like his anarchism and republicanism—a mere literary pose. The situation intrigued me. Here I was standing by the tomb of one of England's greatest poets, talking to a man who had known the Bard from his youth up, but who knew practically nothing of the life-work of this world-renowned singer.

I was glad when he permitted himself to be switched off the vexed subject of theology. "The last time Mr. Swinburne came here," he continued " he asked me to go over the old place with him, and I remember when he got to the highest part of the cliff, he stood right on the edge looking out over the sea with his hat off and his hair blowing in the wind. He said, ' This is the most beautiful spot on God's earth.' Those were his very words. Then he began talking to himself and reciting a lot of poetry. He was quite a long time spouting away up there." My informant paused, then added with a smile, "If I'd have taken up shorthand in my young days, I might have had a poem all to myself ! " Looking down at the grave again he declared solemnly once more, " No, he was no atheist."

Mr. Day accompanied me down the quiet little village street. In an angle of the road he pointed out the exact spot where, one morning, he came across the poet tenaciously sitting astride a literally " prancing steed." The animal was rearing on its hind legs, and doing its best to throw his rider. Mr. Day looked on in alarm, greatly fearing for the safety of the rider whom he expected every minute to see sprawling on the ground.

In spite of Swinburne's splendid horsemanship, the inevitable occurred. One spirited plunge forward and the valiant rider was unseated. Poor Swinburne was shot out of the saddle like a shuttle-cock, and made to feel the uncomfortable contact of mother earth. Fortunately he was unhurt, and instantly picking himself up, was quickly at the head of the now trembling horse. Giving the animal one masterful look in the eyes, he vaulted into the saddle, and with a cheery " Thank you, Mr. Day, I'm all right, but I can't have him showing off here in the street, and I've taught him a lesson to-day, I fancy," he rode off again up the hill with his now sobered steed well under control.

I had to cut the conversation short, for I was due at East Dene, Swinburne's early home, which has now become the seat of a religious sisterhood, the Convent of the Sacred Heart. A strangely anomalous circumstance, it seems to me, that the home of Swinburne's boyhood should have become a nunnery !

A POET'S GRAVE

Lunch was given me in the refectory which, in Swinburne's time, was the library, by Mother O'Brien, the head of the establishment. I found her most amiable and anxious to show me all there was to be seen.

I was taken over the house and grounds. What most impressed itself on my memory was Swinburne's bedroom, a charming apartment looking over the sloping lawn which stretches right down to the sea. Standing at the window one is within a stone's throw of his grave.

On my way back through the Landslip I returned to the grave. The Church was empty now. Not a soul to be seen anywhere. It was deathly still. The cold grey slab, the brief inscription of the name, brought to my mind a thousand memories of the man I had known and reverenced. The poet's own lines on the death of Barry Cornwall, came back to me and it seemed to me that they might well be inscribed over this Bonchurch grave :

> For with us shall the music and perfume that die not dwell,
> Though the dead to our dead bid welcome and we farewell.

Now have I fulfilled the promptings of my heart, my fingers would fain " stray over the lute "; but, alas! I am no " instrumentalist." In writing these last lines my gaze involuntarily travels to the open doorway where I seem to see a familiar figure standing, and to hear, as of yore, the gentle tones of a well-bred Eton schoolboy's voice asking, " May I come in? "

Lightning Source UK Ltd.
Milton Keynes UK
UKOW06f1832120216

268289UK00006B/111/P